The Grace Formula

Discovering God's Promises for a Full Life

Authors: Philip Meinzen and Kim Groshek

Cover design by Danielle Williams

Literary consulting, editing, and formatting, by Clara Rose & Company.

Published by RoseDale Publishing
12121 Little Road, #329
Hudson, Florida 34667

ISBN-13: 979-8-9998796-2-2

Dedication

I am full of gratitude in remembering my redeemed wife, Melede, who was a gift to me. She and our four children and eleven grandchildren are gifts of Grace in my life. I am a wealthier steward than I could have afforded.

Contents

Dedication iii

Contents v

Acknowledgments 1

A Note to the Reader 3

Introduction 5

Meet Philip Meinzen 17

Meet Kim Groshek 21

Faith, Hope, and Love in Action 25

The Fear We Inherited 35

When Your Wallet Reflects Your Heart 45

Grace is not Afraid of Your Numbers 55

Life Decisions Through Grace 63

Grace Before Discipline 73

From Scarcity to Sufficiency 83

The Ripple Effect: How Your Integrity Impacts Others 90

From Stress to Structure 93

Growing What Grace Gives 103

Returning What Grace Gives 115

Trust as a Witness 127

The Power of Stewardship Advocates 139

When Feelings Drive Decisions 147

Faithfulness Over Perfection 157

Grace When the Money Runs Out 165

Getting Back on Your Feet 175

Grace Gives You Enough 185

Provision in Every Season 197
Calm When Money Feels Overwhelming 207
Living Intentionally 217
Grace as Foundation 225
Honor the Heritage of Grace 233
Your 100% Life Starts Now 243
About Philip Meinzen 249
About Kim Groshek 251
More Encouragement 253

Acknowledgments

No father writes a book about Grace without first being humbled by the Grace he has received through his own children. Rachel, Micah, Christa, and Matthew and your spouses and children — you have loved your mother and me with a steadiness and tenderness that has, more than once, carried me when I had little left to carry myself.

You were formed in a home where Grace was the language we were learning together, imperfectly and daily. What moves me most is that the lesson, took. I see in each of you the evidence that Grace does not merely pass through a family — it flows, it deepens, and it multiplies. The way you loved your mother through her illness, the way you have loved me in her absence, and the way you are now pouring that same love into the next generation — that is not your achievement. That is Grace at work, and it is beautiful to witness.

You are, each of you, living proof of the formula this book attempts to describe. I am grateful beyond words to be your father.

"I have no greater joy than to hear that my children are walking in the truth." — 3 John 1:4 (ESV)

A Note to the Reader

This book introduces you to a Person, not merely a principle. The Grace we explore here is not an abstract theological concept or a divine attribute among many. Grace is the very nature and character of Jesus Christ, whom the apostle John described as "full of Grace and truth" (John 1:14, ESV).

When we speak of "Divine Grace" throughout these pages, we are speaking of the Living Word who "became flesh and dwelt among us" (John 1:14). For that reason, every reference to Grace is thereby capitalized. This doesn't necessarily fit editing convention, but we are speaking of the Creator of the universe and the redeemer of all people. For that reason, it deserves capitalization to honor the Source of life.

Every formula, framework, and practical application in this book flows from this central reality: Grace is not only something God gives—Grace is who God *is* in the person of Jesus Christ, who said that He came to give life and give it abundantly or life to the Full. (John 10:10 ESV)

As you read, remember that The Grace Formula is not a method for self-improvement or institutional management. It is an invitation to encounter the Man-God who embodies perfect Grace and Truth, and to allow that encounter to transform how you understand faith, hope, love, and the full and sufficient life He promised and fulfilled on a cross, punctuated in the open tomb, for the Life of the world

The Apostle Paul experienced such a transformation. After encountering the Risen Christ, he was formed to understand the full dimension of a life in the power and promise of divine Grace.

He wrote to the Galatians, "I have been crucified with Christ. It is no longer I who lives in me. And the life I now live in the flesh I live by faith in the Son of God, who loved me and gave himself for me." Galatians 2:20 (ESV)

Introduction

Why This Book Exists

Ever notice how some choices feel easy, while others leave you confused or full of regret? The difference isn't luck—it rests on what actually guides you.

Think of your life like having a GPS for everything that matters: your money, time, abilities, energy, priorities, and relationships. Your character traits are the settings—confident or insecure? Kind or harsh? Humble or prideful? When Grace becomes your number one authority, you discover that The Grace Formula gives you a blueprint that stabilizes and guides your choices toward The 100% Life instead of leaving you stuck, frustrated, or spinning.

A Universal Longing

Every spiritual tradition recognizes the moment when our own guidance system fails us. Buddhists see it as dukkha—the suffering from grasping for control. Hindus understand it as the illusion of Maya. Muslims recognize our desperate need for Allah's mercy. Jews cry out for *chesed*—God's steadfast, unearned lovingkindness. Secular humanists acknowledge the limits of willpower and our need for community and compassion beyond ourselves.

Whatever language you use, the human experience is the same: we reach the end of ourselves. We need something beyond our own effort, our own goodness, our own capacity to hold it all together.

Christians call this power Divine Grace—and the Grace-Flow

Pattern of Faith + Hope + Love describes how that Grace actually reaches us. If you come from another tradition, you might recognize Faith as trust in what we cannot or have not seen, the substance of things hoped for. Hope refuses to believe suffering is final, and Love is the force that connects us to something greater than our isolated struggle. The pattern is universal, even if the source is specific.

What Grace Actually Means

Here's how God's Word characterizes radical Divine Grace for humans: God decides to meet you exactly where you are, not where you think you should be. It's not about doing better or trying harder. Grace shows up specifically in the moments when you have nothing left to prove and nothing left to offer.

But Grace isn't just a single thing. It flows. The Grace-Flow Pattern shows us how Grace actually works: **Grace = Faith + Hope + Love**. Think of it as a current of water that carries you through the chaos of a fallen world.

Faith is trusting that God is present even when you can't see the way forward. **Hope** is believing tomorrow can be different than today. **Love** is both receiving God's love for you and extending it to others—even when you and they don't deserve it, even when you're exhausted or confused.

These three, flow together. When you have faith that God sees you in the Tuesday morning meltdown (the dog threw up, your daughter can't find her science project, traffic betrayed you), Hope begins to whisper that this moment won't define your whole day. And that Hope creates space for Love—maybe you apologize to your daughter instead of staying defensive. Maybe you offer yourself the same Grace you'd give a friend. Is your spouse flourishing in Grace?

The difference between human kindness and Divine Grace is this: human kindness is unreliable and runs out. We get tired, resentful, or busy. But Grace—God's Grace—doesn't fatigue. It doesn't keep score. When you've yelled at your kids, forgotten another birthday, or scrolled through your phone instead of connecting with the people you love, Grace doesn't wait for you to fix yourself first. The flow of Faith, Hope, and Love keeps moving toward you and waits at the door.

The 100% Life @Jubilee Junction™ introduces a biblically faithful blueprint to measure and guide decisions through the lens of the eternal attributes of Grace—flowing through choices that witness to faith, strengthen hope, and glow with love.

Grace's Holy Spirit in the Everyday

Christians believe that God doesn't just observe our chaos from a distance. The Holy Spirit—God's active presence with us—actually works within the mess. This is how the Grace-Flow Pattern℠ becomes real in your life. The Spirit moves Faith, Hope, and Love through and in you, not to instantly fix everything, but to give you what you need for right now and for eternity.

You know that moment when you're about to lose it on your teenager, and somehow you pause? That split second when you choose the kind word instead of the cutting one? That's Love flowing through you—not because you're a good person, but because Grace's Holy Spirit is at work to provide the reset, we are longingly hoping for.

Or when you're drowning in decisions and clarity cuts through the fog—not answering everything, but showing you the next right step? That's Faith being activated. You're trusting something beyond your own understanding.

And when circumstances seem impossible, but you wake up with just enough strength to try again? That's Hope—not optimism, manufactured through Grace. Hope that flows from God's Spirit within you.

For faith leaders who are reading this, you recognize that this justification is possible in the atonement that Grace made possible. Those who, through faith, understand this live the life of sanctification as the Holy Spirit's transforming work through the sacred means of water, word, wafer, and wine soften us, turn us, and redeem us.

Grace is the Justifier who justifies sinners to the standards of a God who is Perfect. Some readers might just refer to it as "surviving." Both descriptions are true. The Grace-Flow Pattern of Faith + Hope + Love is how God's Spirit actually operates, hidden in the mundane moments of your overwhelmed Tuesday.

Good and Bad Traits in Decision-Making

People long for peace, rest, and the freedom to pursue happiness without painful consequences. Here's the truth: something deep inside us is out of tune. From a physical standpoint, health means being born with a strong grasp reflex. What indicates physical strength at birth ironically also exposes an identity crisis during life.

We are creations who have been created in the image of God. God allowed man to know both good and evil, but shielded us from the knowledge of evil until our grasp reflex took over. This pull of death puts mankind on a journey destined to be separated from the God of all Grace.

In such an existence, greed, vice, or virtue will surface depending on how our 'grasp reflex' will lead us to claim or grasp such decisions in our own images and for ourselves. All these factors favor a temptation that bad choices feel easier than good ones. (Ever notice how staying up all night binge-watching feels easier than going to bed on time? Or has your propensity to be a creature of habit defined you rather than your willingness to be versatile?)

This reality also reveals the Power and Promise of Grace—but many don't see this great wonder.

Good (Helpful) Traits

Good traits reflect Grace working in, for, and through us. Bad traits can be canceled or redeemed by Grace, which helps us make thoughtful, merciful, just, and beneficial choices.

Wisdom: Making choices that begin with a reverent fear of Grace comes when our eyes look up to see future opportunities and consequences, not only to you but to others. For example, budgeting your time so you don't burn out from overcommitment. Budgeting your money helps you protect against depletion and increase your supply. The result is that you plan to live in a pattern that is equivalent to the Grace that was given. Besides, it also avoids wasteful decisions.

Fairness and Justice: Sharing resources in ways that are respectful and consider what others need. For example, giving your time and money to help family, friends, strangers, and even enemies consistently and kindly. What results is building trust and teamwork.

Self-Control: Managing your desires so God's provision lasts. Self-control means choosing not to grab everything that catches your eye—resisting that impulse buy, saying no to another serving of food, or turning off the screen when you've had enough. It's the opposite of depletion thinking (I need it all now!). Instead, it's stewardship thinking: “God has given me enough, and I can trust Him for today and tomorrow.”

When you practice self-control, you're actually building three benefits: patience (learning to wait), contentment (being satisfied with what you have), and spiritual devotion (getting stronger each time you choose wisely).

If you're struggling with addictive or compulsive behavior: You're not alone, and you're not beyond Grace. Recognize the pattern. Confess it honestly to the Lord—He already knows, and He's not shocked. Then hear what Grace declares to you: *I forgive you! You are free!* (See John 8:36: So, if the Son sets you free, you will be free indeed.)

Freedom doesn't always mean instant deliverance, but it always means you're no longer condemned. Walk in that Jubilee one choice at a time.

Courage: Taking purposeful risks or standing up for what's good, even when it's hard. For example, learning a new skill even though it costs time and energy now. The result creates new opportunities and growth.

Bad (Hurtful) Traits

These traits distort how we view life and use life's resources. They lead to decisions that hurt us and others.

Greed: Caring only about what you get, ignoring others and the future. For example, blowing all your money on fancy stuff while ignoring savings. The result depletes resources, reduces hope, and breaks trust.

Impulsivity: Making choices without considering risks or trade-offs. For example, binge-watching TV instead of finishing that important project. The result wastes opportunities and creates problems.

Apathy: Ignoring responsibilities and not trying to improve. For example, if you never plan how to spend your money. The result is that things get worse instead of better.

Jealousy: Making choices based on what others have instead of what you actually need. For example, spending money you don't have to look like someone else. This results in wasting resources on the wrong things.

Who Really Owns What?

The more we think we own things, the more those things can end up owning us. So, how's it going? Do you really think you earned everything you have? This isn't meant to make you feel guilty—it's an invitation to see things differently. Who gave you your abilities? Who provided air to breathe and joy to experience? Who designed your eyes to see, your ears to hear, your hands to help, love, and work?

You might say, "My name is on the property title," and that's true for now. But you can't hold it forever. Our management of decisions will either align with the eternal character of Grace, or it won't. As managers of life and life's resources, our actions communicate clear evidence of our identity, values, and priorities—who we really are and what we truly care about.

The clarion voice who brought reformation, Martin Luther, observed that the desire for riches pursues us all the way to the grave. Life's resources and our decisions about them are temporary.

Ownership is only a tangible illusion that ends when earthly life ends. Grace consistently flows through us during our lives, but the ultimate ownership of all life and created resources is Divine.

The Spirit of Grace gives us a repentant and grateful response to share the yoke in our work, our suffering, scarcity or sufficiency, joy, or turmoil. Plus, Grace comforts us with this truth: God owns everything. As the Psalmist writes, *"For every animal in the forest is mine, the cattle on a thousand hills"* (Psalm 50:10 ESV). This means the pressure's off—you're managing what belongs to someone else. This someone is the ONE who fashioned and knit you together in your mother's womb, cares deeply for you, and wants an intimate relationship with you.

The Apostle Paul asks a powerful question: *"What do you have that wasn't given to you?*" (1 Corinthians 4:7 ESV). This challenges the common idea that people truly "own" things, inviting us instead to see ourselves as caretakers—stewards who manage resources to reflect the radiant and warm Glow of Grace.

We are created and called to be stewards of the mysteries of Grace. Understanding how Grace-Flows[SM] offers a Divine path to a full life, with eternal peace and joy in the Lord's Jubilee. Whether you're learning to advocate for your eternal worth or helping others discover theirs, stewardship is your invitation to participate in something bigger than yourself.

What Really Fills the Gap?

Making bright money decisions can help, whether you do or don't have enough, but it can't take away that anxious or empty feeling completely. Only Grace—God's gift to us in Christ—can truly fill that gap.

Here's the encouraging part: Grace is always there for you. It's offered with endless kindness and gives you everything you need to live out your faith, hope, and love in humble and powerful ways. It is balm for our broken hearts and spirits. Grace releases us for the reset and rest that our hearts long for.

When your choices align with Grace—the eternal force that gives and sustains life—something amazing happens. The Holy Spirit empowers your decisions to receive the Lord's Jubilee and create real, lasting, transformed impact.

The Foundation of Everything

In the divine "Economies of Grace," everything is held together by the power of the Creator, Redeemer, and Perfector of all things, and this eternal Grace creates, sustains, and redeems all of life—including yours and mine. This book is an invitation to experience how Grace, our life source, forms all on a firm foundation for a 100% Life, a full life of the Lord's Jubilee! This isn't about perfection; it's about wholeness, freedom, and uncovering your true worth.

Grace has been at work since the very beginning—and it is still at work in your life today. This gift comes from a God who never changes. A God who is Truth itself, revealed in flesh, now clothed in Glory.

When the long-awaited Messiah finally arrived, Grace became one of us—born of a woman. Spoken into being through promises carried by the prophets across centuries—and then spoken directly into Mary's own ears. The Holy Spirit planted the seed mysteriously, convincingly, and powerfully. And from that sacred moment came the One St. John described as *"full of Grace and truth"* (John 1:14)—Jesus, the Christ.

God Himself, in the person of the Son, willingly submitted to the Father's plan. He lived the perfect human life none of us could live. Then He gave His life for ours.

God's Holy Word reveals Jesus as "the Lamb of God who takes away the sin of the world" (John 1:29)—not just our individual mistakes, but the deep patterns of iniquity that keep us trapped. The cycles of injustice make us feel small—the weight of brokenness we carry from generations before us. Jesus, the Christ, takes all of it. And God's work didn't stop 2,000 years ago. He's still taking away sin and iniquity for many. He's still breaking chains. He's still offering freedom.

This is what real love looks like—the kind the Bible calls agape love (or the love of God). It's completely selfless, which is hard to understand. It gives without expecting anything back. It sees the rebellion and systems that have diminished you and says, "No more." It breaks the patterns that have muted your voice and helps you discover that you matter to the Shepherd of all lambs.

Grace invites you to believe in these gifts of faith, hope, and love as you uncover your Jubilee Rest. You don't have to earn it—you can't. You don't have to prove you're good enough—impossible. You don't have to stay stuck in the patterns that have held you back. Grace simply calls you to receive what is already offered: a fresh start, a new identity, and a voice that nurtures and protects—because you are nurtured and protected by the God of Grace. Find your rest in the sanctuary of the Lord's Ark. It is there where Grace, salvation, and Full life flows.

Peace, joy, and contentment can feel impossible to hold onto in this broken world. We see injustice. We feel the weight of our own mistakes. But here's the good news: Divine Grace is the only reconciliation that makes imperfect people right with a perfect God.

The only acceptable sacrifice that could bridge the gap was the Life of God Himself in Jesus—the One who entered our world to take the weight of our consequences, our sin, and our iniquity upon Himself. The Spirit of Grace calls us to walk with Him in an eternal relationship—daily, intimately, faithfully.

When Grace opens our hearts through faith, something remarkable happens. The Holy Spirit plants in us soft and dedicated hearts that see and understand the mysteries of eternal stability, peace, and joy—things the world can't take away.

The formula we're exploring (Divine Grace = Faith + Hope + Love) will offer a blueprint or framework to encourage you to live in such a way that Grace-Flows℠ through you in quiet service and bold witness. Not in words alone, but in how you advocate for yourself and others, how you lead with compassion, and how you break cycles of iniquity with repentant and forgiving love.

You are not alone in this journey. Whether you're finding your calling and/or your voice for the first time or helping others find theirs, remember: You are valued. You are seen. And Grace is here to give you the full life of Jubilee you were meant to live.

We hope this message and practical support systems will encourage you to manage your whole life in light of Divine Grace. Our confidence is that you'll be encouraged by the Biblical blueprint and our curated Grace-Flows journey prepared for you by The 100% Life @Jubilee Junction™.

Meet Philip Meinzen

God's Way of Handling Money

Growing up as a young missionary in India, I thought money was simple: help people who need it—food, medicine, clothes, shelter—the basics. My parents taught me we're here to serve others in God's name and Grace.

Then, at the impressionable age of 12, I moved to America. Suddenly, everything was shiny and new—baseball cards, bikes, gadgets everywhere. The pull was real.

One Saturday night, my simple view was formed into one that required a special relationship. I watched my dad slip real money into an envelope marked "First-Fruits offering."

"Are you giving it away?" I asked.

He smiled. "Philip, it's not mine. It's a gift of God's Grace. I'm just returning the first portion of what was entrusted to me."

That hit me: **money isn't just about spending—it's about trust.**

That moment launched my journey, but I didn't recognize it until later. You see, money carried little intrinsic value to me until I understood why it did. That's when I decided to learn as much as I could about managing money as the culture teaches it. I discerned these teachings in light of God's revealed Truth. Turns out, our stewardship of money reveals our identity and purpose.

Here's the thing: deep down, we all want and need a reset button. A fresh start. Freedom from the stuff weighing us down. St. Augustine nailed it centuries ago—our souls are restless until we find rest in God's Grace.

The Bible reveals the reality of Jubilee—a time when all debts are canceled, and everyone in bondage goes free. That's Grace in action. And guess what? **That reset isn't just ancient history. It's available now.**

Grace-Flows through life like a current. It either moves through our choices—including money choices—or it doesn't. It is a decision that we are enlightened and enabled to make only through faith, by Grace.

I'm grateful I learned these lessons early. Now it's my honor to share them with you in this book.

15 Biblical Truths About Money, Resources, and Grace

One of the free resources found in the appendix section offers a comprehensive list of 15 Biblical Truths about Money, Resources for Individual Stewards. Think of these truths like bowling bumpers. Not rules you follow to earn God's approval—you already have that through Grace. These teachings give you an anchor to help you know the mind of God with reverent fear: wisdom to help you stay in your lane and knock down the pins of life.

When you align your life with these 15 Biblical Truths, you:

- **Recognize** that everything really belongs to God (you're managing, not owning)
- **Return** the first and best portions to honor and reflect the God of Grace
- **Save** wisely and avoid the trap of debt
- **Trust** God with your real daily needs

- **Share** willingly, especially with those who have less
- **Live** with gratitude

That's financial wisdom. That's living in Grace. That's real peace, only found in the Lord's Jubilee.

What I've Learned from Others

I've seen what happens when people miss this stewardship idea. We grab. We chase relationships, stuff, and money instead of trusting God's provision.

I've met people with millions who worry constantly about tomorrow. Never secure. Always unsatisfied or afraid.

I've also met people—rich and poor—who have contentment. They see money as something to manage, not something that manages them. Such people have a magnetic peace.

Over the years, I've had conversations at kitchen tables, in boardrooms, on stages, and in living rooms. I've noticed countless people struggling quietly, sensing there's more for them but unsure how to find it. Some looked successful on the outside but felt empty or unsure inside. Others had passion and purpose but didn't know what to do with it.

I wrote this book because we all need encouragement. When we align our lives with divine Grace, our eyes open. Our voices wake up. We stop sleepwalking and start actually living.

My Story

My journey started in India, where I learned we don't stumble into meaning—we receive it through Grace.

My wife, Melede, taught me even more about Grace during our 44 years of marriage. Early on, she cared for our oldest son, who survived a brain tumor at age two. Years later, at 62, Melede was diagnosed with ALS. Grace enabled her to entrust her life completely to God. Grace gave me the strength to care for her through her decline. Grace kept our children surrounding her with round-the-clock care and hope as she fell asleep and was redeemed by Grace.

Grace is real. Grace is powerful.

This book is a call to action for anyone ready to stop drifting and start living with purpose.

When you handle money with the care and faithfulness of a trusted steward, it stops being a stress. It starts opening your eyes to opportunities and meaning—for you and everyone around you.

Your value isn't defined by your stuff. It's defined by God's Grace, which is always enough.

Let's get started.

— Philip Meinzen

Meet Kim Groshek

Waking to Real Leadership

Have you ever had a moment when things just *clicked*? Like you suddenly understood something big and important? That's what "awakening" means—it's like waking up, not just from sleep, but waking up to something that really *matters*.

That happened to me one day during a quiet walk by the lake. I'd been running businesses, helping people, and doing a lot of things that looked like success. But something was missing. I realized that being a real leader wasn't just about *doing more*—it was about *becoming more*. Becoming someone who leads with purpose, listens deeply, and trusts God even when it's hard.

That's when I started seeing leadership differently—not as a title or a job, but as a way of living.

And I wasn't on this journey alone.

My Friend Sara

Sara might be a lot like you. She is smart, curious, and always thinking about how to make the world better. One day, she said, "Kim, I want to be a leader, but I don't know if I have what it takes." I smiled knowingly and said, "That's exactly where leadership begins—with a question."

Together, we started exploring what leadership really looks like—and we discovered five powerful truths. I call them the 5 Pillars of Dynamic Leadership.

Waking Up to Leadership: Kim's 5 Pillars of Dynamic Leadership.

Leadership isn't about being the boss. It's about how you live your life and how you treat people. It's about doing the right thing—even when no one's watching.

Let's dive into the 5 Pillars:

1. **Integrity – Doing What's Right**
   Integrity means being honest and sticking to your values—even when it's hard. It's like having an invisible badge that says, "You can trust me." Your integrity is your signature; make it clear and true.

2. **Action – Doing Something with Your Ideas**
   Leaders don't just dream—they *do.* They take that next step, even if they're scared or unsure. Don't wait. Take the next faithful step.

3. **Ownership – Taking Responsibility**
   Instead of blaming others, leaders say, "I can fix this." They take charge of their actions and their attitudes. You might not be at fault, but you are always at choice.

4. **Communication – Speaking and Listening Well**
   It's not just about talking, it's about connecting. Great leaders listen more than they speak and choose words that build others up. Speak to connect, not just to impress.

5. **Mindful Pause – Taking Time to Think**
   Sometimes, doing *nothing* for a moment is the most powerful thing you can do. When you pause, you make space for clarity, creativity, and even hearing from God. In your pause is your power.

Leadership isn't just about how you treat people. It's also about how you handle what you've been given—your time, energy, talents, and especially your money.

When you live by the **5 Pillars of Dynamic Leadership**, you:

- **Know Who You Are** – You understand your identity in God.
- **Live Your Values** – You do the right thing, even when it's hard.
- **Communicate with Purpose** – You listen first and speak with love.
- **Make Courageous Choices** – You take action even when it's scary.
- **Lead for Impact** – You make life better for others, not just yourself.

That's leadership. That's influence. That's strength from the inside out.

When I was in upper-level grade school, Phil taught me something that stuck with me for life—he taught me about **Grace**. Not just as a word, but as a way of living. He helped me see that leadership wasn't about being perfect—it was about showing up with courage, listening with heart, and leading with values.

And over the years, he's continued to encourage me—especially when it comes to managing money in a way that honors God. Phil not only helped shape my life, but he has helped many others live with purpose, peace, and generosity.

For me, this book is personal. After years of coaching leaders and launching legacy-driven initiatives, I noticed a consistent theme—so many high-achievers were operating on autopilot. They had the résumé, the recognition, the rewards… but deep down, something was missing. They were *doing* life but not *living* it.

I've always believed that we're not here just to succeed—we're here to awaken to something deeper. Something whole. Something sacred. This book is the guide I wish I had when I began asking bigger questions about identity, fulfillment, and legacy.

Awakening to Grace and The Grace Formula are rooted in the frameworks, stories, and spiritual wisdom Phil and I have both used in our work to help others reclaim their time, energy, and voice. It's about returning to the truth of who you are—before the world told you who to be.

You don't have to wait until you're grown up to be a leader. You can start right now—by making wise choices, helping others, and listening to the voice of Grace.

– Kim Groshek

Chapter 1

Faith, Hope, and Love in Action

When my wife of 43 years, Melede, was diagnosed with ALS, everything I thought I understood about control, security, and stability fell apart. I faced the raw truth: I couldn't fix what was happening. However, I was able to manage my response effectively because of divine Grace. That's when this timeless blueprint for The 100% Life @Jubilee Junction™ came alive within me in a whole new way. This blueprint doesn't make life easier—it makes it full and fulfilling.

As hideous a disease as ALS is, the first appendages to lose functionality were her arms. With that, my dear life's partner and mother of our children was completely dependent on my arms to be hers. I saw this as a high calling from the God of Grace. Together, we grew closer until my four children traveled with her and me, until she fell asleep in the Lord, and Grace redeemed her from age to ages.

An Ageless Blueprint: Grace = Faith + Hope + Love

Grace (100%) = Faith (10%) + Hope (10%) + Love (80%)

Welcome to a timeless perspective on decision-making and stewardship, starting and ending with the Heart of God's Infinite Grace. Managing your life and resources isn't just about numbers—it's about tapping into Grace's power and the promise of the Holy Spirit of Truth and Grace.

Think about guilt, shame, and blame. These feelings prove that our inner hearts are troubled and conflicted. These vices reveal humanity's competing, rebellious nature—we all want to be equal with God, something to grasp for ourselves. The great idolatry of mankind s that we don't only want equality with God, we want to replace Him on the throne. It is the mystery of the ages that, through faith by Grace, we can move toward repentance and the kind of freedom that Grace intends in Jubilee.

Each time we return to this source, we experience freedom in the Lord's infinitely kind Jubilee—a reality where debts are forgiven, and the bound are freed. God's Grace removes the stain of guilt and replaces it with eternal absolution, so we can live in humility, clarity, peace, gratitude, strength, comfort, and joy. Grace is truly the only motivator that can turn drifting lives into focused, faithful diligence.

Understanding the Formula

Grace (100%) = Faith (10%) + Hope (10%) + Love (80%)

Remember that in math, a 'true equation' is correctly balanced. If the equation is not balanced, it is a 'false equation'. This formula is a completely different approach to managing life and resources—where receiving, giving/returning, saving, and spending/allocating are established in Divine Grace. What makes this different? Grace is both the parts AND the sum. The Spirit of Grace produces the faith, hope, and love that give us true purpose, identity, and motivation for life. Our decisions pull together to make our formula either a true equation or a false one. As such, we are living a true life or a false one.

This 100% stands for the eternal character of Divine Grace—the completeness provided by God who IS Grace. The stability we experience when living in harmony and trust is Grace in action, where faith, hope, and love add up to a full, 100% life. The life that Grace came to give. (John 10:10 ESV)

This approach stabilizes rather than creates turbulence. It's different from trying to manage everything through rules, laws, or greed—often just following our own desires or limited interests.

For Christians, Grace is the compelling truth about the Almighty God's gift that reveals to us God's perfect will in Christ, the faithful Son and second Adam, concealed and revealed in the Holy Bible. Yet many believers take Grace's power and promise for granted. If Grace is indeed the Truth, and I believe it is, it should guide our decisions and lives.

If your belief system differs from the Bible's authority, you'll still find encouragement to uncover Grace as a spiritual anchor to clarify your purpose and values.

Grace is universally recognized as a virtue. Regardless of your mental, spiritual, physical, or emotional state, Grace promises comfort to give you eternal peace and joy. Join us as we explore how this framework can encourage, inform, guide, and serve you. It will open your eyes to the goodness of God's Grace for you.

Maybe you're captured by debt, anxiety, or burnout. You can't fix it all, but you can manage how you live through it. This chapter shows how Grace transforms our decisions in the economies of life.

Grace: The Anchor for Life Decisions

Grace is God's perfect, eternal love and commitment to us—because He made us. The God of Grace provides the air we breathe, the forgiveness, mercy, justice, kindness, and liberty, which form the base for a joyful life. Without Grace, we are more apt to chase temporary things that don't satisfy our souls.

Grace brings stability and freedom from anxiety about never having *enough*. It reveals the sufficiency already in your hands and invites you to become someone who blesses others.

Our decisions either help us recognize that we have what we need, or they torment us with feelings of never enough or scarcity. The biblical worldview translates trust in Grace into real assurance and joy about provisions for this life and the next—now and always.

In financial decision-making, Grace doesn't mean being irresponsible. It anchors our management of life and resources in contentment and sufficiency, embracing Grace's sufficient power rather than living in fear of our own scarcity. Grace also gives us the blueprint.

10% Faith: Ownership and Reverence

The first percentage (%) stands for faith—Grace working in us, encouraging us to return willingly and joyfully our first and best to honor the Giver of Grace. It's not about rules or showing off—it's about humility, repentance, and gratitude borne of trust, grounded in divine Grace.

When we return to others in the Name of Grace, it's evidence of our faith. It says, "Spirit of Grace, I trust you as my Provider, Redeemer, and Comforter." When we live with a repentant heart, we honor God's Grace as the Author of Life and Salvation.

Our lives and resources are gifts from our Creator. We're entrusted with faithful use of life's resources according to the baptismal identity and calling of Grace to you. We are endowed in this!

The biblical teachings about first fruits, tithes, and offerings show how God's people have reflected their baptismal calling in returning their best part to honor the Giver. Grace calls each person to find Reconciliation through God's Grace alone. This spiritual gift is what cleanses a leprous heart and changes us to let Grace-Flow in love for our fellow citizens.

Reflecting God's Generosity in the Economies of Grace requires only trust in the Light of the Giver. Such trust is a gift that comes only through the Holy Spirit of Grace. When that repentance and remission takes place, then and only then can our heart be willing, grateful and single-minded. When we yoke our decisions to Grace, returning to God's Kingdom becomes a delight—an act of trust and worship, motivated by faith through Grace.

This kind of faith acknowledges that everything we have is provided for our management, enjoyment, and sharing. Grateful management creates a desire to return the best part to honor Grace, care for others in need, and contribute to sacred purposes in your life and home.

You'll notice throughout this book that we don't use the word *give* when it comes to stewardship. We use the word ***return***. That's not an accident.

When you "give" something, it implies the thing was yours to begin with. But Genesis 1 tells a different story. God created everything—and then He entrusted it to us as stewards, not owners. We arrived after the gift was already here. So, when we bring the first and best portions back to Him, we're not giving God something of ours. We're returning what was always His.

That one word—***return***—quietly confesses the most important truth in this book: you are a steward, not an owner. A mirror doesn't generate light. It reflects the light it receives. That is the steward's calling. And that, changes everything.

A word of caution: If you haven't experienced the joy of returning or figured out your identity and purpose as a bearer of Grace, you may struggle. You might find yourself returning out of guilt, fear, or getting something back. Obviously, that's not faith that equals Grace.

Faith, economically speaking, means knowing your purpose and identity—recognizing you were formed, protected, and ransomed by Grace. This means Grace flows through you.

Material abundance and possessions aren't necessarily evidence of God's blessing; a humble heart is. Understanding and reflecting God's Grace opens Grace's full reconciling power in faith, hope, and love—at 100%.

Grace helps us understand that the Creator keeps ownership while tying Himself to humans and to all creation.

Grace gives everything necessary for life. Salvation has been generously given to us without true worthiness on our part. Because Grace is a gift and we can't pay for it, it's often undervalued and taken for granted.

Living by faith from a repentant heart allows our burdens to be carried by the God of Grace who loves us and gave Himself for us (Galatians 2:20 ESV).

Setting aside this first percentage (%) to reflect faith supports others and invests in the Kingdom of Grace. This affirms our belief in eternal provision and God's lavish love, turning anxiety into eternal contentment, joy, and rest.

Faith clarifies your purpose, identity, and priorities, strengthening your discipline to live within your means. Financial advisors can help navigate details. However, a sure anchor is found in the Economies of Grace revealed in every word of The Holy Bible.

Grace isn't earned—It's given through Faith.

10% Hope: Saving for the Future

The next percentage (%) stands for hope. This includes decisions to build reserves through savings and investments. Hope addresses both expected and unexpected risks and needs, acknowledging life's uncertainties while trusting that what we have is sufficient in divine Grace.

Hope is why God directs us to save and prepare for unknown futures. It's not about hoarding or living in fear but trusting God's provision for today and tomorrow. It's having wisdom to set aside a part, so when life's storms come—and they will—we're ready through Grace's promise and provision.

Consider this biblical illumination from Job's example. After losing everything—possessions, family, health—he didn't blame God. Instead, he said, "Naked I came from my mother's womb, and naked shall I return. The Lord gave, and the Lord has taken away; blessed be the name of the Lord" (Job 1:21 ESV). This is what Grace does when it's both the means and destination of faith, hope, and love.

When we save, it shows our optimism about the future. Godly saving doesn't ever come from fear—We save so that we can be faithful stewards in all our vocations. We save to care for our spouse, our children, our home, our stewardship of the Gospel for future generations. Saving can be a hopeful act, trusting today's provisions while preparing for tomorrow's needs. Living within our means is a disciplined, hopeful trust in Grace's sufficient flow.

This hope-centered approach balances present resources, needs, and future uncertainties for us, our loved ones, and our community. Whether for God's Kingdom work, retirement, emergencies, or long-term goals, hope enables present contentment while building readiness for what lies ahead.

80% Love: Living to Flourish

Most of our decision-making happens in this percentage (%)—the life and resources we use to provide, protect, and share with those closest to us. This covers daily living costs and caring for ourselves and others.

This percentage (%) is about living Gracefully, loving those around us with a love equal to God's Grace, which we've received. It's not about living extravagantly or deprivation—it's about balance. Living in a way that reflects confidence in Grace's sufficiency while wisely managing what's been entrusted to us.

How we manage this (%) reflects our values, priorities, and relationships. When this percentage aligns with Grace, it opens the door for blessing upon blessing. When it doesn't, it becomes a burden.

Love, in money management, means aligning spending with our priority spirit, values, and commitments. It's about living within our means while using our resources to reflect our identity as stewards of Grace, enhancing others' lives, starting with our household. Love also honors hope through saving for future needs and spending on food, clothing, education, healthcare, housing, and experiences that enrich our lives.

Love-based economic decision-making goes beyond mere survival—it's about flourishing. It's about using our resources to nurture opportunity and positive momentum, leading to joy. We use this part to fulfill our and our family's needs, nurturing a meaningful and complete life while upholding the power of Grace.

Managing Money with Faith, Hope, and Love

When we combine faith, hope, and love, we get a complete picture of how to handle money and resources as Grace intended. In a constantly changing world, this approach grounds us with stability and propels us forward with meaning.

Managing money from a faith perspective isn't just about budgets—it's about living in a way that shows we trust Divine Grace to provide. It proves we're called to use our resources in ways that match who we are, what we hope for, and what we are called to carry out.

This approach helps us see that how we spend, save, and share our money is, in reality, a form of worship—a way to honor the 100% that Grace has given us.

The Instability of Control vs. The Stability of Grace

Human nature drives us to set our own limits, always counting and comparing, thus creating instability. This makes managing money feel like a constant struggle. Insecurity drives us to secure our future through our own efforts, leading to anxiety about finances, time, relationships, and security—ultimately harming our spiritual, emotional, and physical well-being, separated from Grace.

But here's the good news: Grace frees us from our shortcomings, weaknesses, and guilt. Under Grace, decision-making isn't about perfection—it's about faithfulness. It's trusting that God's Grace has promised and delivered everything sufficient for our lives, now and forever.

Our role as stewards is to manage well with love, share with the light of God’s generosity through faith, and save diligently in hope. This Grace-grounded approach helps us find stability, contentment and peace especially in uncertain times.

What Does 100% Mean to You?

As we consider the 100% life equation—100% = 10% + 10% + 80%—the first step is defining what 100% means to you. Does it just stand for the sum of giving, saving, and spending? Or does it stand for the integrated wholeness we enjoy through God's undeserved generosity, love, and mercy?

Here's a truth worth pondering: Our stewardship either includes all of life, or it involves none of it.

Too many people think life's choices can be solved through their own efforts alone, without Divine Grace. They miss the Light that shines in darkness.

If you see value in Grace-grounded Strategic Planning™, we confidently affirm that Grace is an anchor for stability, contentment, and joy in planning for personal or organizational transformation. The Economies of Grace offer a stable, reliable approach: **Grace (100%) = Faith + Hope + Love.** Let’s build a community movement of Grace.

Living in and by Grace

Grace-grounded strategic sense thinking goes beyond numbers and behaviors. It helps you integrate purpose and values, aligning decisions with deeper meaning. It's a lifestyle that shifts focus from accumulating things to using resources to serve others and honor the One who breathed Grace into every living thing.

This simple yet profound formula defines a life grounded in

Grace—rooted in faithful stewardship and in God's revealed Love in the flesh; The Full Life (John 10:10 ESV).

10% Faith: Recognizing that everything we have comes from God. He owns it all and governs the affairs of creation and humanity. We trust in His all-knowing, all-present mercy, forgiveness, and approval—gifts we could never pay for but receive freely through His Grace.

10% Hope: Building security for the future by consistently saving a part of what we receive and living within our means. This means spending less than we earn and creating a healthy margin for life's uncertainties and opportunities ahead.

80% Love: Finding true contentment by living with humility, showing mercy to others, seeking justice, and loving kindness deeply. This is where real joy, meaning, and purpose flourish in our lives and communities—not in accumulating more, but in loving well.

Grace's power and promise guide our choices as we journey through life. Whether we are leading a family, living alone, or building something meaningful, we're chosen to distribute resources with focused intention. Grace provides our stability, enabling us to return, save, and live-in ways that embody Grace-Flows of faith, hope, and love.

Economic decision-making can cause stress, anxiety, or division—but it doesn't have to. When grounded in the Grace that formed our world, our choices testify to trust in God's provision and reflect how Grace flows through us.

Stewards are believers who bear the very image of divine Grace. They follow the pattern and power in Grace for life's decisions. Stewardship amplifies what matters most and trims what doesn't. When we are spiritually attentive to our decisions' full context, we recognize that through agape Love in Grace, we find life in all its fullness—beneficiaries of Jubilee!

Chapter 2

The Fear We Inherited

Maya, 35, sat in her car outside the bank for twenty minutes. She needed to open a savings account — a simple step. But every time she reached for the door handle; her stomach tightened.

Her dad never talked about money. Not once. What she learned, she learned by watching: the way he avoided the mail, the way her mom whispered on the phone to creditors, the way the word "budget" made the whole house go quiet. Maya never heard fear spelled out. She absorbed it like weather.

Now she was thirty-five with a decent salary and zero savings. Not because she couldn't. Because somewhere deep down, she believed that money was dangerous — that paying attention to it meant something bad was coming.

She finally opened the door. Inside, she sat across from a young advisor who smiled and asked, “What's holding you back?” Maya opened her mouth to say *nothing*. But the truth came out instead: “I don't know how to trust this.”

The advisor didn't flinch. “That's the best place to start.”

Faith Leader Reflection: Pastor Kevin had seen this pattern dozens of times — congregants who gave with well-intentioned thought on Sunday but lived in quiet financial terror Monday through Saturday. He realized the church had taught stewardship of *what* to do, but rarely *why* the fear was there in the first place. Grace doesn't just correct behavior. It heals the root.

Faith helps me see that life's gifts—time allocated without pay, each breath freely provided, ability, beyond logic, to believe—are all invitations to receive life and resources from God and honor His Grace, which is always enough. The first way I honor this Grace is to let it flow through me: I reflect God's generous, faithful heart in decisions of stewardship.

Returning the first percentage (%) isn't just about money—it's about trusting God's provision when everything else feels uncertain. This practice builds something deeper: a wholehearted commitment to honor God in every part of life. It starts with your wallet and shows up in your estate. It shows up in how you handle life's ups and downs, and flows through the love you give to others.

Key Idea: *Many fears are inherited — and intentional.*

Can 10% Shift Your Center of Gravity?

10% (Faith): How returning first changes what you trust most.

You've been around long enough to see how life has a way of pressuring you into a certain rhythm—especially when it comes to money decisions. By now, you've probably felt both sides of the coin: times when money flows easily and times when every dollar feels precious or vanishing.

It's exhausting, isn't it? The hustle. The grind. The constant worry about whether there will be enough for your future, your family, and your plans.

But here's the thing—money itself isn't good or bad. It's just... money. The problem starts when money becomes the *center* of everything—the sun around which your whole life orbits.

When dollar signs start dictating your decisions, your peace of mind, and your sense of self-worth, something's off balance. That's when you need a different kind of anchor. That's where God's Grace comes in.

The Tax Collector Who Got It

Remember Matthew, the tax collector turned disciple? Before he met Jesus, Matthew was basically the most hated guy in town. Tax collectors weren't just unpopular—they were seen as traitors who lined their own pockets while squeezing money from their neighbors for the Roman Empire.

Matthew knew all about transactions, debts, and credits. His whole world ran on numbers. And yet, Jesus called him anyway. Why? Because Jesus saw past the ledger books. He saw Matthew's heart—the potential for transformation hidden underneath all those receipts.

Your financial life might feel like Matthew's sometimes—full of pressure from every direction, constantly trying to balance everything. But just like Matthew, you can discover God's love and Grace right in the middle of it all.

That's the key: finding Grace within the practical realities of everyday life. It's not about abandoning money or pretending it doesn't matter. It's about learning to navigate it with Grace as your anchor and guide.

Matthew wasn't alone.

Zacchaeus was another tax collector whom Grace transformed. After Grace visited Zacchaeus's home, Jesus said to him, "Salvation has come to this house." (Luke 19:9 ESV)

The Grace Formula: Your Financial GPS

Here's where it gets interesting. Think of your economic life as an equation—a formula where Grace is both the answer *and* the ingredients. Ready? Here it is: **Grace = Faith + Hope + Love**

100% (Grace) = 10% (Faith) + 10% (Hope) + 80% (Love)

At first glance, it looks like a math problem from algebra class. (And if you're having flashbacks to Mrs. Henderson's eighth-grade classroom, take a deep breath—this one is relevant and useful.) But this isn't just numbers. This is a framework that ties together your faith, your hope, and your love with how Grace is hidden in you and how you receive, relate to, and respond to divine Grace.

The formula breaks down like this:

The first 10% represents Faith—what you willingly return to honor the God of Grace. The next 10% represents Hope—what you save in confident preparation for tomorrow. The remaining 80% represents Love—how you live, provide, and flourish in your daily life.

We walked through each of these fully in Chapter 1. Here, the question is what it looks like to actually trust this pattern when money feels like the center of everything.

As we established in Chapter 1, the word we use throughout this book is return—not giving—because stewardship begins with the confession that, nothing we bring to God was ours to begin with. Faith that actually does something.

When 100% Actually Equals 100%

Now, I know what you're thinking. The world doesn't teach any of this. For sure, the world doesn't focus on the 100% given to all of life. You've seen the dominant message out there: accumulate as much as you can, hold onto it tight, build wealth for yourself, and don't worry about others unless there's something in it for you.

But here's what might surprise you: God's wisdom works. Many of today's soundest business principles—things like integrity, fair dealing, and long-term thinking—trace back to biblical teaching. The world shouts about money constantly. God's Word speaks with quiet, steady truth, authority that actually brings peace.

When you align your life with this pattern—where your whole life (100%) breaks down into 10% Faith + 10% Hope + 80% Love—something shifts. Your chaos becomes rest. Your anxiety becomes contentment. Your feeling of "never enough" becomes gratitude for what you have.

> "Faith is not blind; it's grounded in remembrance and reverence, possessing a child-like belief in what is not fully understood."

Two Cities, Two Ways of Living

St. Augustine wrote about this biblical idea of "two cities" that all people live in. One city—the City of God—is filled with people who love God. The other city—the City of Man—is populated by those who love the world. Augustine, a clarion voice of Christian thought in the 4th Century from North Africa, indicated that these two cities were first discernible with the lives of Cain and Abel recorded in Genesis.

You probably recognize which city operates with the values you want to hold. But living in the City of God isn't always easy, especially when the other city's noise is everywhere and deceptively attractive.

The City of Man cares nothing as you worry constantly about your future. It encourages you to chase instant pleasure, to take control and dominate others, to measure your worth by your bank account or the size of your house or job. This city breeds instability and leaves people restless, always wondering if there's enough. Having more things is the desired goal.

But in the City of God? The economy operates differently. It's built on provision, trust, faithfulness, gratitude, humility, peace, contentment, and most of all, on God's divine Grace. These aren't just nice ideas—they're characteristics planted within God's creation and within every child who has been created.

Grace confirms in our restless hearts that God's power is made perfect in our weakness.

Reflection: Faith, if true, equates belief and—it's good work and action, with divine Grace. Even a small act of trusting in the sufficiency of Grace with your first and best can help you reflect Grace's Glow as a 'soul of blessing,' with defined focus, that shifts everything.

Fifteen Biblical Truths: Your Economic Foundation

The God who revealed Himself in Jesus has given us 15 foundational biblical truths for individual stewards about money and resources. Think of these as the building blocks of a financial house that honors the heritage of Grace:

1. Everything Belongs to God: Grace assures us that everything belongs to God (Psalm 24:1ESV). Every breath, dollar, and skill is a gift of Grace. You're not the owner—you're the caretaker.

2. You Are a Steward—A Caretaker: Grace encourages you to take up your role as a steward (1 Corinthians 4:2, Genesis 2:15 ESV). God placed Adam in the Garden "to work it and keep it." Use it wisely, care for it well, and help everything under your care flourish.

3. Grace Provides What You Need: Grace provides what you need (Philippians 4:19 ESV). Notice it says *need*, not necessarily *want*. Grace meets you with the right provision at the right time.

4. Be Content with What You Have: Grace empowers you to be content (Hebrews 13:5 ESV). The world screams, "More! More! More!" Grace whispers, "I am enough."

5. Money Can Trick You: Riches can be deceptive (1 Timothy 6:10 ESV). Money can bless or curse you, depending on your relationship with Grace. What you chase shapes who you become.

6. Take Care of What You've Been Entrusted With: Exercise faithful stewardship (Luke 16:10 ESV). "One who is faithful in a very little is also faithful in much." How you handle five dollars reveals how you'll handle five thousand.

7. Make What You Have Grow: Increase what's entrusted to you (Matthew 25:14-30 ESV). Grace expects us to grow resources boldly and wisely. But there's a difference between wise investment and greedy accumulation.

8. Sufficiency Is Meant for Sharing: Share in the Glow of Grace (2 Corinthians 9:8 ESV). God blesses you not just for your benefit, but so you can do His good work. Sufficient Grace serves a purpose beyond yourself.

9. Return to God Your Best First: Return to God your first fruits (Proverbs 3:9-10 ESV). Offer the God of Grace the first and best of what you have. When Grace's flow is your priority, returning becomes a delight.

10. Return Because You Want To: Return from the heart (2 Corinthians 9:7 ESV). "God loves a cheerful giver." God delights in returning that comes from a willing heart, not obligation.

11. Show Kindness to Those in Need: Grace requires kindness to the poor (Proverbs 19:17 ESV). God calls you to share the generosity of Grace with those who are struggling—love for people who can't repay you.

12. Practice Gratitude: Rejoice in Grace (Philippians 4:4-7 ESV). Gratitude for what you have transforms pity into praise and anchors you in humble dependence on Grace.

13. Don't Let Debt Enslave You: Borrowing obligates your future (Romans 13:8, Proverbs 22:7 ESV). God's desire is for you to live free from that burden. Grace's Flow experiences the reset that leads to Jubilee.

14. Save Some of What You Earn: Save wisely (Proverbs 21:20 ESV). Saving isn't about fear or hoarding—it's about being wisely prepared. Preparation brings peace.

15. Be Trustworthy with What You're Given: Practice faithful stewardship (1 Corinthians 4:2 ESV). God wants you to manage His resources with a willing, faithful, hopeful, and grateful heart. This isn't drudgery—it's liberty in the Lord's Jubilee!

The Bottom Line

These 15 truths form the bedrock of a Grace-grounded strategic approach to money and resources. They're not rules to burden you—they're wisdom to free you. When you embrace these precepts, you move from anxiety to peace, from scarcity to grateful sufficiency, from ownership to stewardship. You discover what it means to live your 100% life—where Grace (100%) = Faith + Hope + Love.

Kenneth Fleck, *Crisis on the Horizon, Rescuing Your Ministry from Financial Meltdown,* AuthorHouse, American Publishing Company, pg. 23-26

Your Next Move

So, what does all this mean for you practically?

It means aligning your heart and spirit with God's character of Grace—seeing your life and resources through awakened eyes. It means recognizing that you're not just a consumer, but a steward entrusted with life and resources that have temporal and eternal implications.

Here's one question to sit with: **How can you stop seeing money as a problem and start seeing it as a way to reflect God's heart?**

When you embrace this approach, something remarkable happens. The more you see Grace at work in your whole life (100%), the more these practices help everything fall into place. Anxiety fades as trust grows. And you discover what it means to live in true freedom—where your whole life actually adds up.

That's the journey we're inviting you into. We've created resources, tools, and encouragement to help you compare biblical wisdom about money with what the world tells you is normal. You'll find practical help to follow Jesus not just on Sunday, but in every financial decision you make. Because when you understand this pattern and, by Grace, live it out, everything changes.

Welcome to a timeless way of thinking about money, resources, and life itself. Welcome to living in the flow of Grace. Our hope for you is that God's Grace will light your path forward.

Chapter 3

When Your Wallet Reflects Your Heart

"In the middle of financial stress and uncertainty, I discovered something surprising: saving isn't driven by fear—it's fueled by hope. Each dollar I put away was really a declaration of trust: *I believe God will provide what I need today, and tomorrow is worth preparing for because His Grace keeps flowing.*"

At this point in your life, saving isn't just bright—it's hopeful. It's saying "yes" to tomorrow while honoring everything that brought you here today.

Caleb's Story

Caleb, 35, was good at looking like he had it together. He wore the right clothes, drove a reasonable car, and always dropped his envelope in the offering plate on Sunday. But behind the scenes, he carried $22,000 in credit card debt — and the shame of it was heavier than the balance.

Every sermon about returning felt like a spotlight aimed directly at him. He started skipping church. Then he stopped reading his Bible. Not because he'd lost faith — but because faith had become a mirror he didn't want to look into.

One evening, a friend invited him to a small group. The leader opened by saying, "If you've ever felt like a failure at money, you're in the right room." Caleb almost laughed. Almost cried. By the end of the night, he hadn't shared a single number. But he felt something he hadn't felt in years: like his worth wasn't attached to his wallet.

Faith Leader Reflection: Pastor Stephen had watched three families quietly leave the congregation after financial struggles. He wondered how many more had simply gone silent. He began asking himself: "Are we teaching stewardship — or are we teaching shame?" The answer changed the posture on how he led.

> Shame doesn't produce change—Grace does. Through Grace, faith transforms how you see life's gifts and respond through gratitude, hope, trust, and love.

The Second 10%: Saving for Tomorrow

This second 10%—the portion you save—isn't just about building a nest egg. It's a way of saying, *I believe in Grace for tomorrow.*

Maybe you look at your life now and think, *I don't have as many tomorrows left as I used to.* That's real. But here's the thing: knowing life is short doesn't make saving less important. It makes it *more* important. Saving creates a cushion that gives you peace of mind as life throws its curveballs.

Picture this: your car needs a major repair, a medical bill shows up, or you get the chance to take that trip you've always wanted. Without savings, these moments create panic, forcing you into decisions driven by anxiety and fear.

Without preparation, decisions made can shackle you. But when you've saved with intention, you respond with confidence instead of crisis.

You've been through enough to know how this works. Maybe you've weathered recessions, job losses, or times when money is tight. You learned to be resilient and resourceful.

Now, saving isn't just playing it safe—it's understanding the opportunity costs of not saving, giving yourself options, and putting your hands on the steering wheel of decision-making, so that your savings intent is, in your view, equivalent to Grace.

As you cross the thresholds of your teens, 20s, 30s, and beyond, your savings priorities look different than twenty years ago. You're probably not saving for a down payment or college tuition anymore. Now it's about healthcare costs, travel while you still can, home repairs, or leaving something behind for the people you love and the causes you care about. Each dollar you set aside moves you toward the life you are called to live—filled with experiences that matter and choices that are truly beneficial, in Grace.

When you consistently save 10%, you're entrusting your future to the promise of God's Grace. This isn't obligation—it's intention, born of encouragement from God's Holy Spirit. You and I are called by our Creator to live, not in scarcity but in readiness, knowing you've prepared diligently and trustingly for whatever comes next. You sense what it means to take responsibility. Since God's Grace is sufficient, you find your '100% Life'- your Jubilee anchored to such lavish love and hope, through faith.

The Power of Perspective

Your mindset changes everything. If you see saving as depriving yourself, it feels like punishment. But when you see it as strengthening, it becomes something entirely different—an act of faithful and hopeful care. You're investing in hope because you know that only those decisions that are anchored to Grace will

"Saving isn't playing it safe. It's saying yes to the provision of daily bread and hope for Grace-Flows and fresh miracles tomorrow."

”

encourage and empower you to handle whatever comes and seize opportunities when they show up.

Here's a simple way to make it happen: set up an automatic transfer each pay period or month. The 10% moves to savings before you can spend it. Over time, you'll watch it grow and realize that every bit actually does count. When available savings reach a threshold of more than 3-6 months of income or earnings, then it may be time to consider how you can increase savings for a longer-term goal.

There's real satisfaction in watching your savings build. It's like planting a garden—you put seeds in the ground today, tend them, and eventually see them bloom. Your savings work the same way. They're proof of your hopes and your plans, growing quietly in the background until you need, and/or share them.

Embracing Change

Life changes, and your savings strategy is likely to change with it. As you move toward retirement, your situation shifts. Maybe you're saving for a slower pace of life, more travel, or helping your kids with raising their family and grandkids with college. Whatever matters to you now, saving promises you the fuel to make it happen.

Saving probably felt like a marathon when you were younger—slow, steady, the finish line far away. Now it's different. It's more like a series of sprints—shorter bursts with clearer goals in sight.

Each financial choice you make today directly impacts how your freedom and happiness tomorrow allow you to bask in the Glow of Grace, from the God who gives all things.

You've started to think like a steward. Rather than earning the right to enjoy what you've built, in humility and reverence, take hold of the Grace that grounds you. In this way, if God so wills, it will be your time to live fully in Grace, knowing that the solid foundation you are grounded in desires a reset, Jubilee, joy, and peace for you and me.

When you "give" something, it implies the thing was yours to begin with. But Genesis 1 tells a different story. God created everything—and then He entrusted it to us as stewards, not owners. We arrived after the gift was already here. So, when we bring the first and best portions back to Him, we're not giving God something of ours. We're returning what was always His.

That one word—***return***—carries the whole theology of stewardship. We unpacked it fully in Chapter 1, and it remains the operating word for what follows.

The Role of Emergency Savings Reserve Funds

As you think about your savings, consider the importance of an emergency reserve fund. This fund is your first line of defense against life's unexpected twists and turns. Financial planning experts often recommend having three to six months' worth of living expenses saved at a minimum. This cushion can provide peace of mind, allowing you to access reserve funds to handle unexpected expenses without resorting to credit cards or loans.

When you have an emergency reserve fund in place, it changes your entire financial outlook. You no longer feel trapped by unexpected expenses. Instead, you face them with confidence, knowing you have the resources to tackle most challenges that arise.

This sense of security is also an outflow of Grace, which reconciles your mistakes and empowers you to make decisions based on what God knows is best for you and your household, rather than what feels necessary at the moment.

The real kicker–Grace builds in you the discipline and courage to not spend everything, but to save as God directed.

Saving with Purpose

In addition to emergency savings, consider setting specific savings goals. Are you dreaming of a mission trip, a trip of mercy and peace, a trip to Europe? Perhaps you want to invest in a new hobby, or maybe you're planning to support charitable causes close to your heart. Whatever your goals may be, establishing them can make your saving efforts feel more purposeful.

Imagine the excitement of seeing your savings grow, knowing each dollar is a step closer to your dreams. Setting aside money for specific aspirations transforms saving from a mundane task into a motivating endeavor. You're not just saving for the sake of saving; you're actively working towards something meaningful.

Celebrating Milestones-Exalting the God of all Grace

When you hit a savings goal, celebrate it. Whether you've reached a specific target or built up your emergency reserve fund, acknowledging these wins matters. It reminds you that saving isn't just sacrifice—it's faithful and hopeful progress.

Your celebration doesn't need to be extravagant, but it should be penitential and exalt the God who gives us all things, in Grace. This posture brings you optimal joy. These small enjoyments keep you motivated and underscore that saving doesn't have to be about denying yourself—rather, it's about creating a life with more freedom to live out your callings, and less fear.

You'll find that listening to the Words of Grace in the Holy Bible will also bring Jubilee into focus.

Building Community

Don't go it alone. Share your savings goals with people you trust—friends, family, maybe a financial accountability partner. Their support matters more than you think. When you talk about what you're working toward, you get fresh ideas and realize you're not the only one trying to figure this out. We hope to build a global network of coaches who have this presence of Grace.

You might discover others have similar goals. Suddenly, you're encouraging each other, swapping tips, and staying accountable. And here's a bonus: the more you talk about money openly, the less awkward it becomes. Financial conversations don't have to be taboo. Sharing your challenges, failures, and wins creates real connection. This is the wonderful paradox of living in the Kingdom of Grace, or as Augustine calls it, The City of God.

Maria's Jubilee Jar Maria started small—just $10 a week. Six months later, she had $500 in her account and something more valuable: renewed confidence that she could actually do this.

Shifting from Scarcity to Sufficiency

We'll go deeper on scarcity versus sufficiency in Chapter 7. For now, the connection to saving is this: every dollar set aside is a small act of declaring that you believe there is enough—and that tomorrow is worth preparing for. That is hope made tangible.

When you approach saving from a sufficiency instead of scarcity mindset, your eyes open to see more clearly. You stop feeling deprived or anxious. You start seeing possibilities. Each dollar you set aside builds hope and says, “I'm ready for whatever comes next."

Throughout this section, we've looked at saving as more than a financial strategy. Saving is an act of Hope. When you set aside money—even five dollars—you're saying tomorrow matters. You're declaring that the future is worth preparing for, even when today feels overwhelming. That's the Grace-Flows pattern at work in your savings account.

Saving as an Act of Grace

Saving requires Faith that there will be a tomorrow to save for. It builds Hope because you're creating options for yourself when uncertainty hits. And it's an expression of Love—for yourself, for your family, for the people depending on you to be stable.

When you save, you're not just building a financial cushion. You're building habits that breed humble confidence. You are confident you have something to draw on when the car breaks down or the medical bill arrives. That confidence changes how you face challenges. You're not paralyzed by every unexpected expense because Grace has given you the Faith to prepare, the Hope to believe you can handle it, and the Love to take care of what matters most.

This is what it means to be a faithful steward of the mysteries of Grace. You're believing and by Grace, partaking in what God has, and is already doing—providing, sustaining, preparing you for what's ahead.

Your savings account becomes a tangible expression of the Grace Flows pattern. It's Faith in action. Hope made practical. Love made concrete.

Every time you choose to save instead of spend, you're saying yes to tomorrow. You're trusting that God's Grace will meet you there, and because God meets you in every day, you're doing your part to be ready as it does.

Key Takeaways

1. **Saving Is Hope in Action**: Saving isn't just bright—it's hopeful. Each dollar you set aside says, *I believe in the provision of Grace for today and tomorrow*, and Grace is preparing you for the life you are called to live.

2. **Build Your Reserves with Purpose**: An emergency reserve fund gives you peace of mind when life throws curveballs. Beyond that, save for specific goals—travel, healthcare, sharing, and nourishing family. When your savings have specific amounts and timelines with measurable outcomes and purpose, it stops feeling like a chore, and you become strengthened.

3. **Shift from Scarcity to Sufficiency**: Stop seeing saving as restriction. See it as opportunity. This hope-filled mindset change, transforms fear into calling, anxiety into confidence, and turns every dollar saved into freedom, increasing restoration waiting to happen.

How can you, by anchoring to Grace, stop seeing money as a leaking pocket or problem and start seeing it to steward choices in Grace designed ways, leading you to a future you are intended to receive?

Chapter 4

Grace is not Afraid of Your Numbers

Maya had been journaling for a week — tracking every dollar, every purchase, every impulse-buy. The notebook was ugly. The numbers were worse than she'd guessed. She stared at the page and felt a familiar wave: *What's the point?*

Then she did something she hadn't done in months. She prayed — not for a solution, but just to say it out loud. "I have $847 in my checking account. I owe $14,000. I don't know what I'm doing. But I'm telling You."

Nothing dramatic happened. No voice, no vision. But the weight shifted — just slightly. She wasn't carrying it alone anymore. She closed the notebook and, for the first time, didn't feel like hiding it.

Faith Leader Reflection: Reverend James had counseled dozens of couples in financial crisis. The breakthrough seldom came from a budget spreadsheet. It came the moment someone said the number out loud — to God, to a spouse, to a counselor. Contrite, trusting honesty was the door. Grace was waiting in the threshold. The final 80% remains sacred ground.

> "The final 80% was where I learned to live presently in each moment with my wife, our family, and our community. Love became the currency that mattered most."

80% (Love): Living to Flourish

Life is more than material things or making money—it's how you use your resources to live, breathe, and connect with others. In this chapter, we're diving into the 80%—the portion of your resources that represents Love and connection. This is where your priorities either conflict, or by Grace, beneficial action happens. How you actually manage this 80% reveals a lot about your worldview, values, priorities, and relationships.

Love in Economic Decision-Making

At its core, love-based economic decision-making is about using your resources to reflect what truly matters to you. It's about ensuring that your spending aligns with your income, but more importantly, your top values. As you look at your economic choices, ask yourself: How can I use my income or wealth to make a positive impact? What truly honors the Grace first given me, and brings joy and fulfillment?

In a world that constantly bombards you with messages about needing the latest trends and gadgets, it's easy to forget what really brings happiness. You may feel pressure to conform to societal expectations of success, but remember: true fulfillment comes from meaningful connections to whatever Grace stands for in you, not only material possessions. Your economic choices should reflect this understanding.

Living Within Your Means

Living within your means is crucial. It's about making choices that support your immediate needs and align with your long-term goals. You might think budgeting is boring, but consider it a tool for freedom rather than a constraint. When you budget wisely and track the progress in detail, you learn that, even if you don't seem to have enough, you receive sufficient Grace, which empowers you to enjoy life fully and freely, without the burden of debt or guilt hanging over your head.

Take a moment to reflect on your spending habits. Are there areas where you could cut back or reallocate? Maybe it's that daily coffee run or subscriptions you don't really use. By being mindful of your expenses, you are freeing up resources to invest in experiences that truly matter—like living out your vocations (callings) with others, pursuing service and hobbies, or supporting causes you care about.

Living within your means doesn't mean depriving yourself; it's about making intentional choices that bear the image and Glow of Grace. This might look like cooking at home more often, choosing to spend on experiences rather than things, or prioritizing saving for a future goal—whether that's a buffer for unexpected costs, a home or automobile, or even starting your own business.

Enhancing the Lives of Others

One of the most rewarding aspects of managing your economic decisions with Love is the ability to share your resources with others. Think about the impact you can have on the people around you. Whether it's helping a member of your household, a friend in need, supporting a local ministry or charity, or treating your family to a special meal, these acts of Grace create ripples of positivity in your communities.

Here's what shifted for me: when I started seeing my financial choices through the lens of love, money became less about transactions and more about relationships. Suddenly, I wasn't just paying bills or balancing a budget—I was connecting with people. Whether it's helping a friend in need, supporting a ministry or social services doing good work, surprising someone with a thoughtful reflection of God's generosity or treating the family to an experience we'll remember, every dollar became a chance to say, *You matter to me.*

The money you steward can do something powerful: create moments that outlast any purchase. Think about it—years from now, will you remember the stuff you bought, or the weekend trip where everyone laughed until they cried? The best use of your resources isn't always another thing to own. Sometimes it's helping a niece pay for college. Sometimes it's showing up with groceries when a friend loses their job. Sometimes it's gathering everyone for a weekend away where phones get put down, and conversations go deep. These are the investments that compound in ways no bank account ever will.

Flourishing Through Economic Choices

When you think of the percentage (%) to share Love as an opportunity to flourish, you begin to see your economic choices as more than just numbers on a page. Your spending can create a life filled with joy, adventure, and meaningful connections.

This mindset encourages you to view money as a tool for growth and happiness. When you discipline your spending to guard priorities, your values and experiences related to possessions, begin to percolate toward a full life.

Use your resources to explore what it takes to strengthen current bonds, pursue new endeavors, or invest in building God's Kingdom of Grace. These are the things that manifest your obedience and disciplines, enrich your life, and lead to lasting fulfillment.

Aligning with Your Values

To fully embrace Love in your economic management, it's important to regularly evaluate how your spending aligns with your

Grace or authority. Here are some questions to guide your reflection:

What do I truly value in life? Think about what matters most to you—your sacred beliefs, relationships, personal growth, experiences, or passions. Make sure your spending reflects these values. In other words, align your Love with the Grace that give Love and life.

How can I adjust my spending habits to better align with my priorities? Determine a way to look at your recent expenditures. Are there areas where you can redirect your funds toward things that bring you joy or support your goals? Writing your plan and tracking mitigates overly emotional decisions.

What small changes can I make to ensure my economies reflect my values? This could mean setting aside a portion of your income for the ongoing good work of Grace, saving for experiences instead of things, or simply being more aware of where your money goes.

Love, Grace, and Hope in Your Economic Journey

Love, the agape response, integrates into your economic journey when our hearts are circumcised into Christ's death, approaching others as yourselves and marinating your heart with servant ready Faith and Hope that doesn't disappoint. These gifts come from Grace.

Grace is about God's infinite kindness to you. We have a higher calling to be kind to others and to ourselves. Economic setbacks are bound to happen—whether it's an unexpected expense or a job that doesn't pan out. Rather than berating yourself for mistakes, treat them as learning opportunities that will help you grow. Recognize that in Grace, you are never alone.

Hope encourages you to dream big and keep moving forward. You might not have everything figured out right now, but that's okay. Trust that each economic decision you make, no matter how small, contributes to your future, which, when aligned with Grace, allocates Hope in God's Grace.

Finding Meaning in Your Spending

As you think about the 80% of your resources, focus on viewing necessities as a priority and finding meaning in how you spend. Approach your economic choices with intention and diligence.

Consider making a list of experiences or contributions that bring you joy. Maybe it's funding a friend's art project, going on a spontaneous trip, or treating your family to a special dinner or service project. When you prioritize meaningful experiences over material possessions, you nurture a life filled with joy and connection.

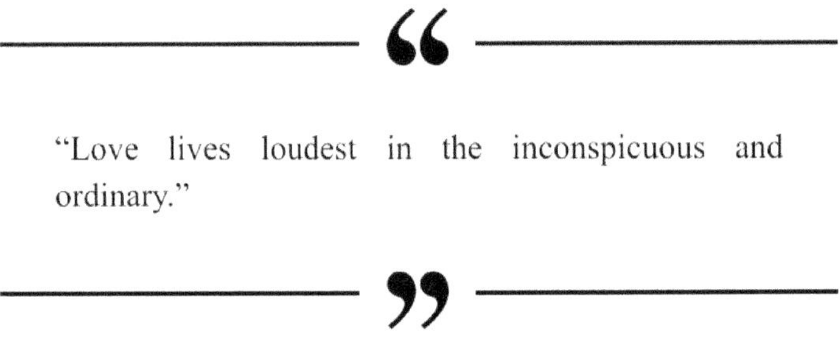

Planning a Heritage of Love

You can start thinking now about the heritage you aspire to and build. How do you want to be remembered? What impact do you want to leave behind for your God, family, friends, and communities?

Economic choices made today can lay the groundwork for a lifetime and a heritage of Love. Focus on nourishing relationships and building up the work that you believe is good and that you care about. The values and experiences associated with your priorities will become the foundation of your heritage. You want the people in your life to remember not just what you had, but how you made them feel, think and the impact your stewardship has in their world.

The Ripple Effect of Love-Based Spending

When you practice love-based economic decision-making and management, you inspire those around you to do the same.

Your choices can influence your friends and family, encouraging them to embrace a similar approach to life's economic decisions and all of life's resources that honor the heritage that you have been given.

This ripple effect nurtures a culture of kindness and connection. By living out your values through ageless economic wisdom, you contribute to a broader movement of kindness and mutual support.

Your Grace-grounded commitment to sharing and enhancing the lives of others can inspire positive change, create a community that honors connection over consumption, reconciliation and redemption over guilt, blame, and 'mine' living.

Key Takeaways

Align Spending with Values: Love-based economic decision-making ensures that your expenditures are managed to reflect your deepest commitments. Assess how your economic decisions align with what truly matters to you and snuff out the competing commitments.

Flourish, Not Just Survive: Approach your life and life's resources with a mindset of helping all under your care to flourish, to be everything that they or it was created for. The best way to do this is to save and not exhaust every resource you have been given that can help create margins that precipitate joy, opportunity, and positive change in your life and the lives of others, including loved ones you care about.

Create a Heritage of Love: Your economic decisions today can add up and multiply into a lasting heritage. Focus on fanning into flame the faith within. This, along with the lessons of experiences and relationships that nurture agape Love, the Love that is equivalent to Grace, and provide meaningful connection, glowing with purposeful impact on your communities.

Spending is essentially a vote where every dollar is a small declaration: *this is what I'm for.* The question is whether your spending ballot and your beliefs are actually voting for the same things.

Chapter 5

Life Decisions Through Grace

I stopped seeing decisions as just data points. Grace redefined my approach: decisions became moments to steward faithfully (aligned to Grace and life flowing towards Jubilee.

Caleb had said, "I trust God" his whole life. He meant it—mostly. But when it came to money, trust felt like a bumper sticker—words on a surface with nothing underneath.

His small group leader suggested one simple experiment: for one week, before making any purchase over $50, pause for thirty seconds and ask, "Do I need this, or do I want this?" No guilt. No rules. Just a pause.

Day one was hard. Day three was harder. By day five, Caleb realized the pause wasn't just about money. It was a tiny act of trust—a repentant moment where he was helped to believe that he didn't have to grab everything now. That there would be enough.

It wasn't a transformation. It was an inch. But it was the first inch he'd taken in trust in years.

Pastor Daniel had seen countless "commitment cards" signed at the end of emotional services. But commitment without practice was like a muscle that never got used. He began teaching his congregation that trust wasn't a decision made once—it was a habit built daily, one small choice at a time.

What Does Grace Mean to You?

In Christian belief, Grace is the Character of God given freely to people who are the crown of creation—The Almighty's favor and approval that we don't earn and don't deserve.

It's shown when He saves sinners through God's own sacrifice. This gives us a divine reset and blessings in this life and forever. If you believe differently, then perhaps Grace has other meanings for you, both as a word that describes things and as an action.

Grace as a thing (noun):

1. **The indispensable source of life,** without which we could not survive.

2. **A short prayer of thanks** said before or after a meal. Like when someone says, "Let's say Grace before dinner."

3. **A Grace period**—extra time officially given to pay a bill or follow a rule. For example, "The bank gave me a three-day Grace period."

4. **A title for royalty or church leaders**, like "His Grace, the Duke" or "Your Grace."

5. **The Three Graces**—in Greek mythology, three beautiful goddesses (Aglaia, Thalia, and Euphrosyne) who represented charm, Grace, and beauty.

Grace as a describer (adjective):

1. **Simple elegance in movement**—like "She moved through the water with effortless Grace."

2. **Courteous goodwill**—like "At least he had the Grace to admit his mistake."

Grace as an action (verb):

1. **To honor something or someone by being there**—like "She Graced the sport for two decades before retiring."

But for our journey together, we're exploring something deeper than definitions. We're discovering what God's Grace really means in our lives.

Discovering Grace in Economic Decisions

Welcome to a journey where economic decision-making meets Grace. In this context, Grace represents the God-given, undeserved life and resources that we're called to manage so we can accomplish the vision of our highest purpose and related aspirations.

At every age, it's easy to get caught up in the hustle and bustle of everyday life, viewing material resources and wealth as a simple equation of how much you earn versus how much you spend. But what if true economic decision-making goes beyond just numbers? It's about redefining your life and life's resources through Grace, embracing a mindset that nurtures your spirit and resources of time, talent, and treasure.

Trust is built on the foundation of Grace—not declared; trust grows through practice, not pressure.

In this chapter, we'll explore Grace in economic decision-making. You'll learn how to redefine what "wealth" means to you and understand how your economic decisions reflect what Grace means to you. As stewards, you'll discover how to live in what St. Augustine called "The City of God"—a place where people love God who provides sufficiency and redemption. Let's dive in!

Redefining Life and Life's Resources Through Grace

Our very existence—mind, body, and spirit—requires us to receive and manage material goods of time, talent, and legal tender.

Resources are often perceived in material terms: a nice car, a spacious home, designer clothes, or a full bank account. However, it's crucial to redefine material resources through the lens of Grace.

Grace isn't just about financial sufficiency; it's about appreciating the blessings you already have and using them in line with your spiritual and emotional priorities, applied within your vocations (callings) to enrich the lives of those around you while enriching your own life.

The Illusion of Material Wealth

You might feel pressured to keep up with the lifestyles of others, especially with social media showcasing curated images of success and luxury. It's easy to fall into the trap of comparing yourself to those who seem to have it all. But remember, the illusion of material wealth can be deceiving. Just because someone appears economically successful doesn't mean they are happy, fulfilled, or living a life of purpose.

Embracing Resources from Grace

Redefining life and life's resources—including our wealth, wisdom, and work—starts with gratitude. Instead of focusing solely on what you lack. Grace makes it possible to shift your perspective to appreciate what you already possess: your faith, your abilities to earn and manage, your health, relationships, opportunities, and experiences.

This mindset of Grace nurtures gratitude, allowing you to see the beauty in the everyday moments and seasons of life.

Ask yourself: What are the things I value most in my life? Perhaps it's your relationship with God or the support of friends and family. Pursuing your passions or the freedom to explore new opportunities becomes joyous rather than burdensome.

When you identify your core purpose and values, you'll find that resources and wealth are more than just money; they're the richness of your life's experiences, relationships, and the reasons and ways your material resources are applied.

"Grace doesn't eliminate logic—it harnesses it."

”

Nurturing a Grace-grounded Mindset

To nurture a Grace-grounded mindset toward life and life's resources, consider these practices:

Practice Gratitude: Start a gratitude journal. Each day, write down three things you are thankful for. This simple practice shifts your focus from scarcity to sufficiency reminding you of the resources (daily bread) already present in every moment of your life.

Limit Comparisons: Reduce your time on social media or unfollow accounts that make you feel inadequate. Instead, surround yourself with people and content that inspire you and align with your highest values and encourage your faith, hope and love, in Grace.

Focus on Experiences: Spend your resources on experiences that bring you joy, rather than material possessions. Invest in restoring hope and faith with others, building savings, strengthening relationships, traveling, or pursuing hobbies where Grace-Flows—these ways to share the light of God's image within will enrich your life and the lives of others around you far more than things ever could.

By redefining wealth and resources through Grace, you can build a more fulfilling and purposeful life, one that reflects your values rather than society's expectations.

Grace Framework: Economic Decision-Making

Economic decision-making emphasizes responsibility and care in managing life and life's resources. At its core, it's about understanding how to make your resources of time, talent, and money reflect Grace while remaining aligned with your values. The equation of economic choices consists of three key components: inflows, outflows, and impact.

Inflows: Earning with Intention

Your inflows are not just a number; they reflect your skills, passions, and hard work. As you move toward your tomorrows—whether career, home care, education, or retirement—it's essential to approach earning with intention. Consider not only how much money you hope or expect to earn, but also what kind of work will bring you fulfillment.

Choose Purpose Over Paycheck: While it's important to earn a living, prioritize jobs that align with your passions and higher values. Finding work that excites you can lead to greater job satisfaction and growth opportunities.

Invest in Yourself: Education and self-improvement are vital components of building your income. Consider taking courses, attending workshops, or seeking mentorship in areas that interest you. The more you invest in your skills, the more you increase your potential to earn.

Diversify Your Income Streams: Look for opportunities to create multiple streams of income. Whether it's freelancing, starting a side initiative, or investing, having diverse income sources can provide economic security and flexibility.

Outflows: Spending with Purpose

While earning money is crucial, how you spend it matters just as much. The way you allocate your resources reflects your values and priorities.

Budget with Intention: Create a budget that reflects your goals and values. Allocate a portion of your income to savings, investments, and meaningful experiences. By being intentional with your spending, you can cultivate a lifestyle that aligns with your vision.

Prioritize Needs Over Wants: Distinguish between your needs and wants. While it's okay to indulge occasionally, focus on spending your resources on things that genuinely enhance your life, such as worship, health, housing, food, education, and experiences.

Practice Conscious Consumerism: Be mindful of where you spend your money. Support businesses and brands that align with your values, whether that means shopping locally, choosing sustainable options, or supporting companies with ethical practices.

Impact: Planning a Heritage Transfer Plan

The final component of the economic decision-making equation is impact. How can your financial choices create a positive influence on your life and the world around you?

Agape Love flowing through you: Consider incorporating the notion of philanthropy. However, since this is much more than sharing 'filio' (love as in friends) love, I like to introduce the more accurate term "agapethy"—into your economic vocabulary. Whether it's donating to a cause you care about, volunteering by returning time, or supporting local initiatives, your contributions not only reflect the flow of Grace, they help achieve a collective vision.

Share Knowledge and Wisdom: Use economic decisions to apply your knowledge and the wisdom that is given supernaturally and through experiences to help others. Mentor a friend or colleague who is struggling with their life's situations, or create content that equips others about economic literacy and living in correlation to Grace.

Plan a Heritage of Grace: As you develop your resources, think about the heritage you want to provide. How do you want to be remembered? Whether it's through charitable planning, mentorship, or community involvement, aim to leave a positive, restoring, and reconciling impact.

Understanding this equation of economic decision-making encourages you to take control of your resources and make decisions that reflect your values, ultimately leading to a more meaningful life that balances our understanding of Grace with our actions as managers.

Living in God's City

Now that you've redefined wealth through Grace and understood the equation of economic stewardship, you can better understand what it means to live in God's City.

The concept symbolizes a place of sufficiency, gratitude, community, redemption, and purpose—a Grace-breathed state of mind where you recognize that you are part of something larger than yourself.

The Sufficiency Mindset

Finding Purpose in Your Journey

When you align your financial stewardship with your purpose, you create a powerful impact on your life and the lives of those around you. Reflect on your passions and how you can integrate them into your financial choices.

Explore Your Passions: Take time to discover what truly excites you. What activities make you lose track of time? What ignites a fire in your heart? Pursuing your passions can lead to opportunities for income, fulfillment, and community connection. Find your calling and follow.

Set Purposeful Goals: Establish financial goals that align with your values and purpose. Whether it's saving for a meaningful experience, starting a business that reflects your passions, or enhancing the community of saints, ensure that the Grace of God inspire your goals.

Celebrate Progress: As you work toward your financial goals, celebrate your progress along the way. Acknowledge the steps you've taken, no matter how small, and allow yourself to enjoy the journey.

Trusting the Journey

Living in God's City requires faith—faith is a gift of God's Grace. Such faith sees self, humbly yet treasured; it also sees others this way, within the greater plan for your life. Embrace the idea that you are on a journey, and trust that every experience that contributes will be blessed to your strength and humble confidence.

Let Go of Control: Understand that you won't always have everything figured out. Embrace uncertainty and trust that the right opportunities will present themselves at the right time.

Practice Mindfulness: Stay present in your financial journey. Instead of worrying about what might happen in the future, focus on the actions you can take today to create a brighter tomorrow.

Seek Guidance: Surround yourself with mentors, friends, and resources that align with your values. Don't hesitate to ask for help or seek advice as you navigate your financial stewardship.

In this chapter, we've explored the beauty of discovering Grace in financial stewardship and economic decision-making. By redefining wealth through Divine Grace, understanding the equation of financial stewardship, and embracing the sufficiency of God's City, you can navigate your finances in a way that reflects your values and enhances your life.

A Question to Reflect On

As you move forward in your journey of financial decision-making stewardship, ask yourself: **How can I redefine my relationship with wealth to align with Grace and purpose?**

Remember, your financial journey is uniquely yours. Embrace the opportunities ahead, and let Divine Grace guide you as you navigate the world of economic decision-making and finances.

Chapter 6

Grace Before Discipline

For those who live by faith, Grace allows us to stand at a crossroads where stewardship feels less like a burden and more like an exciting invitation to see.

Maya had tried every system. The envelope method. The app. The spreadsheet a coworker swore by. Each one lasted about two weeks before she felt suffocated and quit.

She was sitting with her aunt—a woman who had raised four kids on one income and never seemed stressed about money—and asked, “How do you do it?”

Her aunt laughed softly. “I stopped trying to be perfect first. I let God remind me that I was already enough—and *then* I figured out the money stuff. Not the other way around.”

Maya blinked. She had been trying to earn her peace through discipline. Her aunt was saying peace came first—and discipline followed naturally.

That night, Maya didn't open a budget app. She opened her Bible. It felt like the first real financial decision she'd made in years.

Faith Leader Reflection: Principal Erik had seen burnout in his own school ministry team—people who followed every rule but lost their joy. He began to wonder if the school and church had accidentally taught people to earn God's approval through obedience. Grace, he realized, wasn't the reward for doing things right. It was the starting point for everything.

As you navigate life's complexities, true leadership as a steward isn't just about being first in line or climbing the ladder. It's about building trust, encouraging growth, and serving those around you. Grace-grounded decision-making is more about God working through us than about our own achievements.

Welcome to Grace-Grounded Stewardship—a way of living that can reshape your identity, build gratitude, and strengthen your community.

In this chapter, you'll:

- Discover your identity in God's Grace
- Learn how God's generosity flows through faith, hope, and love
- Understand how God works through you in your daily roles
- Build communities where everyone can flourish

As you step into this transforming space, let's explore how becoming a servant leader can change your path and the world around you.

Your Identity is Hidden in the Christ of Grace

"For in Christ Jesus you are all sons of God, through faith. For as many of you as were baptized into Christ have put on Christ." (Galatians 3:26-27 ESV)

Understanding your identity in Christ is a journey of discovery. You're not just someone with dreams—you're a steward of sacred gifts, talents, and resources God placed in you. Our lives reflect Grace's image. God's Word calls this a 'good deposit' (2 Timothy 1:14) entrusted to you.

Think about it this way: Every skill you have, every relationship you build, every opportunity you pursue plays a vital role in a larger story. As (1 Peter 4:10 ESV) says, *"Each of you should use whatever gift you have received to serve others, as faithful stewards of God's Grace in its various forms."*

A Moment of Reflection

Take a moment. What gifts has Grace given you? Maybe you're great at connecting people, sparking creativity, or encouraging others with your words.

Recognizing that all of life is a Gift of Grace is your first step toward embracing your identity as a steward. Your purpose in Grace goes beyond personal success or failure. It's about honoring God for sufficiency, whether in opportunity or challenge, while enriching others' lives.

When you align your identity with Grace as a steward of the mysteries of God, you become aware of opportunities to serve and influence. Consider how you can serve at home, in your neighborhood, or at work. Maybe through your job, family time, unpaid service, or being a supportive friend.

Every act of encouragement, love, and service places you in a role as a ministering spirit. This is what living out our calling as stewards looks like: setting the foundation for effective servant hearts, as a steward, disciple, and leader.

The Power of God's Promise for Gratitude

Being generous isn't only about money. It's a complete approach to life that reflects God's Grace through faith, hope, and love. It includes your time, energy, and effort. You might feel overwhelmed by responsibilities and commitments, or overrun by stress about having or not having enough, or the shackles of pressure when we don't think we have enough, or want more than we can afford. Faith, through Grace, helps us have hope to realize that God's Grace lives in you. The presence of Grace is a powerful answer to life's pressures.

The Ripple Effect of Seeing Need and Sharing Willingly

You're at a coffee shop and decide to pay for the drink of the person behind you. This simple kindness can create a ripple effect, inspiring them to do the same for someone else. This is an example of one small way that God's Spirit works through us—accepting that our Creator hides Himself in us has the power to transform moments into movements.

Having a "good eye" to see others' needs and living as a 'soul of blessing' is living God's Generosity in the way that God's Word describes it. No wonder the generosity that reflects Grace, as hidden in us, is contagious when shared! It enriches those you touch and contributes to your own growth. When you return yourself first to the Lord and then others, in keeping with your faith, you receive joy, peace, and a stronger sense of freedom and community.

Embracing a Single-Minded, Merciful Willingness to Share

To follow the generous spirit of Grace, consider:

Start Small: Don't wait for excess resources. Help the poor, serve without pay for an hour a week, listen to a friend, or share your skills with someone who needs advocacy and guidance. Try using cash if you struggle with spending boundaries—start at home!

Be Intentional: Make being a "soul of blessing" part of your daily routine. Write an encouraging note to a coworker or offer your appreciation or skills to a local nonprofit. Remind people they're treasured by the God who made them in His Grace.

Reflect on Impact: Regularly think about how God's Generosity through your decisions affects others and yourself. This deepens your understanding of stewarding God's mysteries and reinforces your sense of identity and purpose.

Building Community Through Grace-Filled Stewardship

As you embrace your identity in Christ and adopt His generous nature, following as a disciple and steward naturally leads to stronger community ties. A flourishing community that is grounded in Grace requires and reflects trust, collaboration, and shared purpose.

Essentials of Effective Servant Leadership

Lead with Humility

Servant leadership means putting others first. It's about listening, valuing input, and recognizing that everyone has something to contribute. When you lead with humility, you create space for collaboration and innovation. In this way, you orchestrate rather than control.

Ask yourself:

- How can I listen better to my team and others?
- How can we communicate better?
- What steps can I take to encourage and equip others?

Build Trust

Trust is your community's foundation. To build it:

Be Transparent: Share your vision and decision-making process openly. Honesty builds trust and encourages shared stewardship as heirs of eternity.

Listen Actively: Engage with community members and validate their contributions. Listening builds relationships and improves decisions.

Share Stories: Stories inspire connection. Share your successes and challenges to illustrate a shared vision.

Case Study: Darlene's Stewardship Reset

Darlene felt lost in her role until a Grace-Discovery Assessment helped her rediscover the blockage that kept her from her purpose and identity as a steward of Grace. By understanding her unique Grace-Flows and blockages, she found renewed passion for serving her community.

The Impact of Visioning

Strategic visioning emphasizes the big picture, helping you consider long-term impact. Vision is a shared reality—it's the impact of "mission accomplished."

Vision can only be fulfilled when we work together. Use visionary language instead of focusing on "needs." Leading with your needs often feels manipulative. Everyone has needs. Instead, encourage your team to think about how their work contributes to a larger vision—something we can only do together.

Engagement is Key

Involving Your Team: Hold sessions where everyone can share ideas. Group brainstorming builds creativity and innovation.

Involve the Entire Community: Once you've crafted the vision, continually ask members to share their stories and evidence of Grace through faith, hope, and love.

Emphasizing Humility and Versatility: While vision provides direction, stay open to adjusting strategies as things change. Being versatile and resilient is key.

Develop Specific, Achievable Plans: Distill many ideas from visioning sessions into manageable priorities. Then create a plan to accomplish optimal engagement activity that is grounded in Grace.

Key Principles of Board Leadership

As a servant leader, guiding your board:

- Establish Clear Roles: Define responsibilities to prevent confusion and ensure everyone knows their roles and contributions.
- Encourage Collaboration: Build an environment where board members support each other through regular meetings and open communication.
- Monitor Progress: Develop systems for tracking progress toward agreed-upon agreements and goals. Regular assessments and reporting maintain accountability.

Functioning as a Fit Fiduciary

Your responsibility extends to ensuring your organization's resources are managed wisely, ethically, and faithfully—both to keep public trust and honor the heritage of Grace. This includes:

Financial Integrity: Maintain transparency in all financial dealings. Regular reports help stakeholders understand financial health and trajectory.

Resource Allocation: Make informed decisions about distributing resources, prioritizing what aligns with your mission.

Risk and Opportunity Management: Identify potential risks and develop mitigation strategies. Also assess opportunity costs—what you give up for decisions made.

Stewardship Attitudes & Assessments

God saved us - and it wasn't because we did anything to earn it or because we were good enough. He saved us simply because He's merciful and loves us perfectly. He washed away our old life and made us completely new through the atoning sacrifice of His own Son, the First Fruits of all creation. And He didn't hold back either - He poured out His Spirit on us generously through Jesus Christ, our Savior. Because of His Grace, we've been made right with God, and now we're His children with the incredible hope of living with Him forever. (Paraphrase of Titus 3:5-7 ESV)

When you begin to anchor your life in Grace, then you begin to see that "You are not managing scarcity—you're stewarding sacredness and sufficiency."

Building a steward's heart and mindset is essentially the work of the Holy Spirit in faithful servant disciples and leaders. Here are three key cultural markers that will be present:

- Glowing with God's Gratitude and Grace: Glow with God's generous Grace by worshipping in the house of the Lord, sharing your life, resources, and expertise, inspiring your team to do the same.
- Encourage Accountability to Grace: Build a culture where team members have 'good eyes' and begin, with the Power of Grace, to take their place through regular check-ins and evaluations.
- Celebrate the Impact of Grace-Flowing in You: Regularly evaluate your own walk as a steward and disciple. In repentant humility, identify areas for improvement while giving honor to the God of Grace by receiving setbacks and successes as opportunities to exalt God's Grace.

Managing Key Outcome Factors

Identifying and stewarding key factors that fuel and protect alignment with the mission is crucial:

- Define Success: Work with your team to determine what success looks like. Ask everyone to paint a vision of potential related to your mission and vision.
- Develop Metrics: Establish clear metrics to evaluate progress. Make sure all metrics align with Grace's mission. For example, when a Christian School sets its primary metrics for a discipled steward as the outcome of their ministries, then this can be defined as Grace Himself defines it, and it can help create not only mission alignment but also achieve vision.
- Celebrate Achievements: Acknowledge milestones to boost morale, praise the Lord for the work of Grace in us, and consecrate and reinforce commitment to your mission.

Motivating Accountability & Faithful Decision-making

- Setting Clear Expectations: Communicate expectations of Grace as Faith, Hope, and Love clearly to provide a faithful and encouraging framework, with exit or pivot plans if needed.
- Providing Encouragement and Support: It's important to remember that accountability, if real and relevant, will always be correlated to support. Offer resources, training, and mentorship to help your people and team reach their goals.
- Creating a Grace Environment: Build an atmosphere where team members feel valued. Regularly express gratitude for their contributions and create a path to orchestrate avenues for constant constituent listening, so each can feel heard. With an authentic and accurate feedback loop, the community is strengthened as those who lean in increase

Conclusion: Embracing Your Role as a "Grace-Flow" Servant Leader

As you embrace your journey as a "Grace-Flow" Servant Leader, remember it's not just about achieving goals. It's about serving others and building a culture of Grace, faith, and grateful stewardship.

Key Takeaways

1. Uncover Your Mission's Promise: Recognize and use your unique gifts to serve your community in compelling, authentic ways.
2. Build Gratitude: Embrace a mindset of seeing others' needs and being energized to encourage, inspire, and connect.
3. Live and Lead with Integrity: Commit to leading with integrity, compassion, and a clean heart for service in faith, hope, and love.

By adopting these perspectives of Grace, you'll enrich your life and become a catalyst for change in your own life and in your community. Your journey as a "Grace-Flows" Leader has just begun—embrace it with confidence and Grace!

Chapter 7

From Scarcity to Sufficiency

What if There's Enough? Grace Beyond Scarcity

Alright, let's dive into something super important but often overlooked—**financial ethics and integrity**. When you think about money, what comes to mind? Paychecks, bills, maybe even that vacation you've been saving up for.

But what about the deeper stuff, like the moral and spiritual implications of how you handle your money and how your decisions align with and reflect your values? Sounds heavy, right? But stay with me, it's not just about following the rules.

Caleb made $62,000 a year. By most measures, he was doing fine. But he lived as though the next paycheck might be his last. He hoarded coupons, compared prices on everything, and felt genuine anxiety at the grocery store.

A coworker invited him to lunch — a simple deli down the street. Caleb ordered the cheapest sandwich and spent twenty minutes calculating how much he'd spend if he ate out once a week for a year.

His coworker watched him quietly, then said: "You know you're allowed to have enough, right? You don't have to work for the right to feel okay."

Caleb didn't have an answer. But the question stayed with him for weeks. Slowly, he began to notice how scarcity thinking had crept into everything — not just his wallet, but his relationships, his faith, even his sense of purpose. He started asking a new question: *What if there's enough?*

Faith Leader Reflection: Brother Robert counseled a family who returned faithfully but lived in constant financial fear. He realized sufficiency wasn't about the number in the bank. It was a spiritual posture — a belief that God's provision was real, not theoretical. Teaching that truth was as important as teaching any budget principle.

It's about being transparent, honest, and ethical (beyond reproach) in everything you do, especially in how you manage financial decisions. *Let your light so shine before others* . . . (Matthew 5:16a ESV)

This chapter is all about unpacking what it means to approach financial decisions with ethics and integrity. You're going to see that financial stewardship isn't just about making smart money moves—it's about living in a way that aligns with your beliefs, reflects your values, and honors God's Grace in every financial decision you make.

Sufficiency is spiritual maturity, not financial excess. "Integrity is doing the morally and spiritually honest thing when fear tells you to lie."

The Weight of Financial Decisions

Let's start with the big picture. Every time you make a financial decision, whether it's as simple as grabbing your daily coffee or as major as signing off on a mortgage, there's a ripple effect. It's easy to think that your choices only impact you, but the truth is, they go much further. Your financial decisions affect your family, your community, your future, and yes, even your relationship with God.

Take a moment to pause and think about this: Are your financial decisions based solely on what benefits you, or are they rooted in something bigger? Are you thinking about how your choices impact others? Are you being transparent and honest with yourself and others in how you ground decisions to steward money?

It's tempting to cut corners or tell yourself that "no one will notice" when it comes to finances. But every decision, no matter how small, builds up your character. And when it comes to stewardship, being aligned and grounded in the Character of Grace is everything.

The Moral and Spiritual Truth of Money

Money in itself isn't good or bad—it's neutral. It's how you prioritize it and what you do with it that carries moral weight and spiritual gravity. You've probably heard the phrase "money is the root of all evil," but that's a common misquote. The full phrase, from the Bible, is *"For the **love** of money is the root of all kinds of evil"* (1Timothy 6:10a ESV). Paul isn't saying money is evil. He's saying *loving* money—being obsessed with it, letting it control you—that's the problem." It's that obsession with prosperity in material possessions, that blind pursuit of more, that can lead you down the wrong path.

> Just as "life begins to grow" from a seed or root, so all kinds of evils emerge and grow from love of money.

So, what does it mean to approach your finances morally and spiritually?

Well, it's about more than just avoiding shady business deals or staying out of debt. It's about making choices that reflect your identity and values, showing compassion, and always keeping a contrite heart, recognizing that from dust we came and to dust we will return. Such moral and spiritual honesty at the forefront of your financial life is a prerequisite to balancing your life to the Grace Formula.

Here's an example: Imagine you're doing well at your job, and your employer accidentally overpays you for one month. Do you keep the extra money and chalk it up to good luck, or do you point out the mistake and return what isn't yours? This scenario might seem like a no-brainer for some, but when faced with it in real life, it can feel like a moral dilemma.

Ethical decisions like this one pop up all the time, and how you handle them says a lot about your integrity. The real challenge is consistently choosing a repentant posture, recognizing that we bear within us the Glow of Divine Grace. In this light, honest humility, even when it's inconvenient or when no one is watching, becomes a backbone.

The Importance of Transparency

Let's talk about transparency for a few seconds. In the world of finance, transparency is about being clear and open about your financial dealings. Full disclosure is important for owners to receive from custodians. Yes, it is even baked into the laws of most free enterprise cultures.

If this is true among us created beings, how much more is it true for our relationship to the Owner of our world, life, resources, and immortality? That's why the Grace Formula is grounded in the Grace of God's perfect Spirit, whose intent for you and me is agape Love. This is the faith, hope, and love that is equal to divine Grace. This formula applies to how you manage your personal budget, how you handle your business, how you lead organizations, or even how you share with others and steward relationships.

Why is transparency so important? It builds trust. Whether it's with your family, your employer, your constituents, or your community, being transparent about your financial situation creates a foundation of trust and reliability. People trust you more when they know you're honest and upfront about your finances. Be honest, but be wise. Transparency doesn't mean oversharing—it means being open with the right people at the right time.

But transparency isn't just "about being honest with others—it's also about being honest with yourself. When was the last time you sat down and really looked at your spending habits? Are you spending money on things that matter to you, or are you swiping your card mindlessly? It's so easy to lose track of where your money is going, but if you want to be a good steward, you've got to keep yourself accountable. If you could benefit from a Grace-grounded advocate or coach, let your leaders know.

'Oh Christ, cover me in the robe of Your righteousness. Grant me honest shame and true repentance, Amen.' (Isaiah 61:10 ESV)

”

Building a Foundation of Integrity

Integrity is like the backbone of ethical financial decisions. It's related to those purpose and identity core values that keeps you grounded in what's right, even when it's tough. It's what pushes you to make decisions based on precepts and principles, not just on what's convenient or profitable.

When it comes to finances, having integrity means these characteristics and more:

- You reflect the character of Grace as you live in faith, prosper in hope, and love in Grace
- You don't cheat on your taxes. *". . . therefore, render to Caesar the things that are Caesar's, and to God the things that are God's"* (Matthew 22:17ff ESV)
- You're upfront about your financial situation with your family or business partners.

- You don't make promises you can't keep, financially or otherwise.
- You pay your debts, even when it hurts.
- You give credit where credit is due.

Here's the thing: Having integrity with your money isn't always easy. In fact, it can be downright challenging. But it's during those tough decisions—when you're tempted to take the easy way out—that your true character shines through.

One thing to keep in mind is that integrity is a long game. It's about doing the right thing, even when the reward isn't immediate. Sometimes, choosing to act with integrity might feel like you're losing out. Maybe you missed out on a quick buck because you didn't take part in a shady deal. But in the long run, integrity builds a reputation and a peace that money can't buy.

Making it Real: Financial Integrity in Daily Life

Okay, so how do you actually live this out when you're standing in the checkout line or staring at your bank account at midnight? Here are some practical ways to build financial integrity into your everyday rhythm:

1. **Track Your Spending:** Look, this isn't exciting. But honesty starts with knowing where your money actually goes. Use an app, a spreadsheet, or good old pen and paper—whatever works for you. You can't be transparent with yourself if you're avoiding the numbers.

2. **Set Clear Boundaries:** Ever made a purchase you regretted five minutes later? Boundaries protect you from those moments. Create a budget that reflects your real life—not the Instagram version—and stick to it. It's not about restriction; it's about freedom.

3. **Avoid the Bondage of Debt:** Some debt might be unavoidable—medical expenses, a mortgage, student loans, maybe a car. But living within your means isn't about

depriving yourself. It's about not borrowing from your future self to fund today's impulses. It's financial integrity in action, protecting you.

4. **Practice God's Generosity:** Here's the thing about returning—it recalibrates your heart. When your decisions reflect God's generosity, money loses its grip on you. You remember it's a tool, not a trophy. And that shift? It changes everything.

5. **Get Accountable:** Find someone you trust—a financial coach, a mentor, a friend who won't let you off the hook—and talk honestly about your goals. Accountability isn't about judgment; it's about having someone in your corner who helps you stay true to what matters most.

Why Honesty Matters in Stewardship

Here's the foundational Truth: everything you have—your time, your talents, your money—ultimately belongs to God. You're managing it, not owning it. That's why honesty isn't optional in stewardship.

Think about it this way: If someone handed you their wallet or portfolio and said, "Watch this for me," would you be careless with it? Of course not. You'd guard it, use it wisely, treat it with respect that protects the owner's interests—because it's not yours.

That's stewardship. Your money, your resources, your decisions—they're all on loan. And when you handle them with transparency and integrity, you're honoring the trust God's placed in you.

Living with financial integrity isn't about avoiding guilt or staying out of trouble. It's about gratitude. It's about saying, *You've trusted me with this. I'm going to handle it well.*

In the hardest seasons, small decisions tested my integrity. Grace demanded truth—even when it was uncomfortable.

The Ripple Effect: How Your Integrity Impacts Others

Living with financial ethics and integrity doesn't just affect you—it impacts the people around you and can create a ripple effect in your community. When you choose transparency over shortcuts, when you live honestly even when no one's watching, people notice. Your kids see it. Your friends feel it. Your coworkers respect it.

Think about your family, your friends, or even your co-workers. When they see you handle your finances with integrity, it inspires them to do the same. And when more people start living that way, it creates a culture of trust and honesty that benefits everyone.

And slowly, something beautiful starts to grow. A culture of trust takes root. Honesty becomes contagious. People start thinking, *If they can live that way, maybe I can too.*

That's the power of integrity. It doesn't just protect you—it transforms the people around you.

Key Takeaways

1. **Ethics in Every Decision:** Every financial choice carries weight—from the coffee you buy to the career you choose. When you let integrity guide your decisions, you're not just managing money. You're living out your values and honoring God with what He's entrusted to you.

2. **Transparency Builds Trust:** Being open about your finances isn't about oversharing your bank statements. It's about living in alignment with your values and creating a foundation of honesty in your relationships. When people know you're trustworthy with money, they trust you with more.

3. **Integrity is the Long Game**: Financial integrity might not give you instant results. You won't always get the applause or the shortcut. But over time, it builds something money can't buy—a reputation rooted in character and a life that reflects God's faithfulness.

How can you bring more transparency and integrity into your daily financial decisions—and what ripple effect could that create in your family, your workplace, or your community?

You've just dived below the surface, into what it means to handle money with ethics and integrity. Now comes the real work: living it out.

But here's the good news—you don't have to be perfect. You just have to have a contrite spirit. Willing to make the repentant and honest choice when it's inconvenient. Willing to be transparent when it's uncomfortable. Willing to let your financial decisions align with and reflect what you truly believe. Every choice is an opportunity to live with integrity. Every decision is an opportunity to steward well what God has placed in your hands.

So, breathe in the Breath of Life. You've got this. And remember—you're not managing your resources alone. You're partnering with the One who gives all good things.

Let this wisdom guide you as you navigate your financial journey, keeping in mind that every choice you make, when anchored to Grace, will reflect the glow and flow of God's goodness. You will have peace, joy, and freedom when Grace-grounded values light your path, guide your steward walk, and comfort you.

As Grace hearkens, 'Go live it out joyfully. Your Light has come!'

Chapter 8

From Stress to Structure

You're about to explore practical tools and Biblical teachings that will help you live out your calling as a steward in God's Kingdom of Grace. Making money decisions is a big part of stewardship—it's a light that glows as Grace shines through your everyday life.

In this chapter, you'll dig into the Grace-Flows Design Toolkit, learn why it matters to reflect Heaven's Grace in your money choices, and check out interactive tools that make financial decisions accessible, simple, and even fun for the whole family. (Yes, we said *fun*. Stick with us here.)

Maya's Story

Maya and her sister hadn't spoken in three weeks. The argument had started innocently—a question about splitting the cost of their mom's birthday trip. But it uncovered years of unspoken resentment: Maya felt she always paid more. Her sister felt Maya always judged her spending.

Maya sat on her couch, staring at her phone. She could text something sharp. Or she could do something harder.

She called. Not to win. Just to say: "I think we've been afraid to talk about this. Can we try again—without keeping score?"

Her sister was quiet for a long moment. Then: "Yeah. I think so."

The conversation that followed wasn't perfect. But it was honest. And by the end, they'd made a plan—not just for the trip, but for how they'd talk about money going forward. Together.

Faith Leader Reflection: Reverend David had seen marriages end not because of debt, but because of silence. The couples who made it through financial hardship weren't the ones with the best spreadsheets—they were the ones who learned to talk. He began dedicating a full small group session to teaching couples *how* to have the money conversation, not just *what* to discuss.

The Grace-Flows Map

Your journey toward solid financial stewardship starts with the Grace-Flows Map—a clear and helpful processes that emerges from the Grace Formula. It provides an **overall visual framework or system for what you see**. Mini-courses will soon be available to offer Grace-grounded help with money and life decisions, helping you line up your financial choices with what the Bible teaches.

Picture this: you're sitting down with a Grace-Flows Ambassador or Facilitator who *gets* you—someone who listens to understand your soul, and your unique situation, values, and dreams. This advocate will encourage and equip you to make decisions that are equivalent to the Grace that you have been given. When finances are seen not as a headache, but as a gift—a way to serve others and honor God's Grace, then you are on the road to the Lord's Jubilee.

The Grace-Flows Design Toolkit

At the core of the Grace-Flows Design Toolkit is learning about God's Power working through His all-powerful, all-knowing, all-present Grace. This is your opportunity to gain essential (and eternal) knowledge about managing life wisely—your spirit, intellect, body, emotions, daily tasks, money, time, abilities, and relationships. Think of it as a crash course in earning, spending, saving, investing, and returning—all through the lens of faith, hope, and love in Divine Grace.

Your experience will help you create a Grace-Flows Journey that fits your values and lines up with your Grace. This designer considers the material facts about your income, expenses, and goals, making sure your decisions align with how you view faith, hope, and love through Grace. You'll learn practical strategies to tackle challenges while building an attitude of gratitude, humility, and trust in God's infinite kindness and mercy that leads to freedom.

Seeing God's Grace in Your Money Choices

Think about it: every choice you make with your time, money, or talents can actually point people to God. Your resources aren't just about buying stuff or building up savings—they're chances to show what God is like through how you use them.

Look at how Jesus handled money when divine Grace walked the earth. He was all about being generous, caring for people, healing hurts, and staying focused on what really matters forever—not just piling up earthly stuff.

When you start seeing Jesus in your money choices, something shifts inside you. The way you use what you have becomes a way to show what you treasure, honoring God and showing others what Grace looks like in action.

What you buy shows what you value. How you save shows you're being wise. What you return shows your faith and love at work. Every single choice becomes an opportunity to bring glory to God and help build His Kingdom of Grace right here on earth.

Grace Discovery, Design Toolkit, and Journey

As you work through The Design Toolkit, you'll get Discovery Reports. This takes your Discovery Reports and a free assessment showing where Grace is flowing and where is may be blocked, and how this affects other areas of life. These tools can encourage and equip you to see with good eyes and to consider your situation in Grace to get from where you are to where you, by Grace, want to be.

Create a Grace-Flows Design Toolkit—*a personalized planning reality check and pathways to encourage you to order and reflects your values in the Power and Promise of Grace.*

As you examine your income, expenses, and savings habits to get a clear picture of your financial landscape, it helps clarify and spot where you want to make changes or where your opportunities and risks are.

Imagine sitting down with a set of questions asking you to think about what really matters. You might see questions like: *What is my Guiding Authority? How can my decisions align with the 100% I've been given? What are my financial goals for the next year? How can I make my spending match my income and values? In what ways do I show God's Generosity in my willingness to share Grace with others-with my voice, my hands, my money?*

As you answer these questions, you'll create a clearer picture of where you stand financially and what matters most in life. This process helps you make informed decisions that either reflects your confession to honor God's Provision of pure Grace upon Grace, or it speaks anemically about the Grace that we are taking for granted.

Money Lessons the Whole Family Can Use

One unique thing about the Grace-Flows journey is its recognition that the whole person and whole family are given to you to flourish. Financial stewardship isn't just your solo journey—it's an adventure with the ones you love that can impact generations to come (Actually, it's pretty amazing when you think about it).

Get your kids involved in real conversations about budgeting, saving, and returning. By modeling healthy financial habits, you equip them with the tools they need to navigate life's challenges. Try involving them in family budgeting sessions or encourage them to set aside part of their allowance for returning. Simple practices like these reinforce the importance of a humble spirit and generous heart that reflects God's character.

As a family, you can create a stewardship plan using the Grace-Flows Design Toolkit that outlines your shared goals and commitments. This might include a family tracking system for income and earnings, a budget that sets aside resources for returning, savings, and spending, lessons on how money works, specific returning goals for community service, and regular family discussions to reflect on God's Grace and adjust your plans.

Jason's family was always stressed about money until they started using the Grace-Flows Tracker at their family table.

The simple act of tracking together brought focus, calm and allowed everyone to get on the same page.

By working together, your family can build a culture of stewardship that honors God and reflects His love in your household and community. And honestly? It beats arguing about money in hushed tones after the kids go to bed.

Beyond Your Family: Christian Schools

"The Treasure" curriculum for Schools and High Schools is for students to experience stewardship in the Economies of Grace. The curriculum, built on a platform developed by the National Council on Economic Education is retrofitted with spiritual objectives for each lesson to amerce students in the practical nature of God's Word related to managing money and resources of time, talent and treasure as a steward of the Gospel.

This decision-making approach encourages and equips the youth to learn and apply these Grace lessons through Christian and Home Schools. Educators and parents will find integrated lessons about decision-making that align with biblical teachings of Grace, helping students build real financial literacy rooted in faith, hope, and love.

Imagine a classroom where students learn not only about economics but also about stewardship—how to manage life's resources. They're taught the importance of using what they have wisely, understanding the value of hard work and savings, protecting our neighbor and recognizing why returning matters as you reflect on everything that was given to you first.

The Treasure curriculum will equip teachers with the tools they need to pass on The Grace Formula effectively. By weaving biblical economic teachings into their curriculum, schools are preparing the next generation to approach money decisions with a timeless perspective. This builds a culture of stewardship that extends beyond the classroom into students' homes and future careers. (Basically, we're helping kids avoid the "I have no idea what I'm doing with money" panic that hits most of us in our twenties.)

Imagine a Grace-Flows Community

As you work through the precepts, principles and practices in the Grace-Flows Journey, consider becoming part of a larger community where the glow of Grace warms hearts and opens the door for liberty. Whether comprised of individuals, families, schools, churches, or membership organizations, those committed to living in harmony with the Economics of Grace will be a catalyst for unlocking the power of Grace.

Imagine being part of a community where you can share your experiences, challenges, and victories in a no-pressure, no-guilt, no-obligation stewardship network. The Grace-Flows Journey provides a supportive network that encourages accountability and collaboration. You'll find friends and advocates who hear your values and aspirations, helping you stay focused on your faith during the journey.

Connect with your community's Grace-Flow discerned leader. They're dedicated to encouraging and equipping individuals and families to embrace their calling as stewards.

Connect with us: GraceFlows.org

By joining the Grace-Flows community, you'll not only grow in your understanding of stewardship but also engage in a movement where Grace-Flows in honor of God and transforms lives—now and eternally.

Grace Thrives in Structure, Not in Stress

Here's something most people get backwards: they think structure creates stress. More rules, more systems, more tracking—sounds exhausting, right? But here's the truth that flips the script:

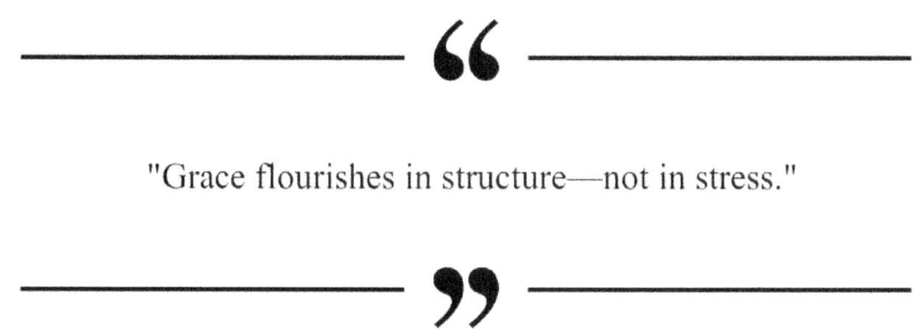

"Grace flourishes in structure—not in stress."

Think about it: When you have no plan for your money, every spending decision becomes stressful. Should I buy this? Can we afford that? Where did all our money go this month?

That's stress talking—and stress drowns out Grace.

But when you have structure? When you've already decided where your money goes, what you're saving for, and how much you're returning?

Suddenly, those daily decisions get easier. The structure creates space for Grace to flow. You're not constantly worried or second-guessing yourself. You're free to share God's Generosity when you see a need. You can say yes to what matters without guilt or panic.

Structure isn't about being rigid it's about being intentional and ordered. It's the difference between reactive living (where life happens *to* you) and Grace-filled living (where you make choices that reflect a trust in Grace).

Building Your Structure

As you move forward, here are practical steps to build the kind of structure where Grace can thrive:

Start with the coordinator. Reach out to express your interest. They'll provide resources and help connect you with resources, an ambassador or facilitator who can guide you through building your personal structure.

Complete your Steward's Survey. This self-assessment shows you where you are right now—no judgment, just clarity. You can't build a good structure on shaky ground.

Work through the interactive tools and worksheets. These aren't busywork. They're tools that help you think through your financial habits and set goals that actually match your values. This is where you start building your structure—one decision at a time.

Make it a family initiative. Share the program with your family. Talk about how you can work together on Grace-driven stewardship. When everyone knows the plan, there's less conflict and more cooperation (Trust me, "because it's in the budget" is a lot less stressful than "we can't afford it" when your kid asks for something).

Show up for workshops and mini-courses. Look for opportunities to attend events offered by the Grace-Flows community. These gatherings deepen your understanding and give you practical tools. Plus, you'll meet other people building their own structures—and learning you're not alone in this? That's encouraging.

Build accountability. Set regular check-ins with your Grace-Flows Ambassador to review your financial goals. Join a small group that discusses what it means to be faithful with money. Share your goals with trusted friends or family who can encourage and support you. The power of accountability strengthens your resolve and helps you stay on your journey as a steward of God's Grace.

The Path Ahead

As you wrap up this chapter, take a moment to reflect on the tools and resources being prepared for the Grace-Flows Journey. You're not doing this alone. You have a supportive network and resources to help you flourish as a recipient and manager of God's blessings.

Remember, stewardship is a journey of transformation—a process of aligning your heart with God's purpose and learning to see the Grace of Christ in every financial decision. As you engage with The Grace Formula, be open to the ways God is calling you to grow and serve.

Three Main Takeaways

Structure Creates Space for Grace: The Grace-Flows Journey provides personalized coaching that helps you build financial structures aligned with biblical truths. When you have a plan, you're free to be generous, intentional, and responsive to God's leading—without the constant stress of reactive decision-making.

Structure Works Better Together: The program equips you with tools to involve your whole family in building healthy financial structures. By creating a family stewardship map and teaching biblical principles, you build a foundation where Grace-Flows freely for generations to come.

Structure Needs Support: Joining The Grace Formula or Grace-Flows community provides the accountability and encouragement you need to maintain your structures. When life gets messy (and it will), having others who share your values helps you stay committed to the structures where God's Grace liberates—not the stress where it suffocates.

Question to Reflect On: What is one specific financial decision you can make this week that aligns with your values and reflects your gratitude for divine Grace?

In the next chapter, we'll dive deeper into the transformative impact of stewardship on your life, your resources, and the lives of others. Together, we'll explore how your commitment to living as a steward can create a ripple effect that extends far beyond your immediate circle, touching lives and advancing God's Kingdom of Grace.

Chapter 9

Growing What Grace Gives

Let's be honest—investing can feel scary. Maybe you look at your bank account and think, "I'm just trying to pay the bills. How am I supposed to invest?" Or you hear friends talking about stocks and mutual funds, and you feel lost. You're not alone.

Here's what we want you to know: investing isn't just for people with lots of money or fancy business degrees. It's for anyone who wants to build something for the future—even if you're starting small.

And the best part? You can invest in ways that match who you are and what you believe in.

In this chapter, we'll break down investing in plain language. We'll talk about how to grow your money while staying true to your values. We are not going to use confusing jargon. We hope to offer only practical steps you can actually use.

Caleb had set a goal: pay off $22,000 in debt in twelve months. By month two, he'd paid off $400 and felt like a failure.

His accountability partner — an older man from church — listened to Caleb's frustration and then said: "You paid off $400. That's $400 more than you had paid off last month. That's not failure. That's movement."

Caleb wanted to argue. But something about the simplicity of it landed. He wasn't behind. He was moving. Slowly, imperfectly, but forward.

He began tracking not the debt total, but the small wins: the day he didn't swipe the credit card. The week he cooked every meal at home. That morning, he returned $20 to a coworker's fundraiser without guilt. Each one was tiny. Together, they were becoming a new story.

Faith Leader Reflection: Pastor Mark had watched too many congregants set ambitious financial goals and quit when the progress felt invisible. He began preaching about faithfulness in small things — not as a consolation prize, but as the actual mechanism of change. The Bible didn't promise overnight miracles in finances. It promised that faithfulness in the small was never wasted.

Why Investing Matters

Before we talk about *how* to invest, let's answer the bigger question: *Why should I even care about investing?*

Maybe you're thinking: "Isn't investing risky? Shouldn't I just keep my money safe in a savings account?" We get it. Saving feels secure. But here's the hard truth: just saving money won't get you where you want to go. Remember that if your posture is completely defensive, you won't have the growth potential needed for the effects of Inflation (when prices go up over time). This economic reality slowly eats away at your savings. That $100 bill you saved today. In ten years, it won't buy as much as it does now.

Investing gives your money a chance to grow faster than inflation. It's how you build financial margin—that breathing room we've talked about throughout this book. It's how you prepare for the future, whether that's retirement, your kids' education, or simply being ready for life's surprises.

And here's something that might surprise you: you can invest in companies and priorities that reflect what you believe. Whether you care about faith, caring for the creation, or treating workers fairly, there are investment options that line up with your values.

Investing isn't just for the wealthy—it's about planting what you believe in, even in small amounts.

The Basics of Investing

Let's start with the fundamentals as your starting place. Once you understand these concepts, investing will make a lot more sense, and you will find these basics to guide your decisions.

1. Risk vs. Reward and Time-Horizons

Every investment involves two things: risk and reward. Risk is the chance you could lose money. Reward is the potential for your money to grow.

High-risk investments (like buying stock in a single company) can bring big rewards—but they can also mean big losses. Low-risk investments (like savings bonds) are safer, but they grow more slowly.

The key is finding what works for *you*. Ask yourself: How would I feel if my investment lost 20% of its value tomorrow? If that thought makes you sick, you probably want safer investments. If you can handle the ups and downs, you might be comfortable with more risk.

Here's another important factor: time horizon. This is just a fancy term for "When will I need this money?"

Short time horizon (less than 5 years): If you're saving for something soon—like a down payment on a house—stick with safer investments. You don't have time to recover from big losses.

Long time horizon (10+ years): If you're investing for retirement or something far in the future, you can usually handle more risk. You have time for your investments to bounce back from temporary drops.

2. Diversification

You've heard the saying: "Don't put all your eggs in one basket." That's diversification.

When you diversify, you spread your money across different types of investments—stocks, bonds, maybe some real estate. This way, if one investment does poorly, others might still do well. You're not betting everything on one thing.

Think of it like this: If you only invested in one restaurant and it closed, you'd lose everything. But if you invested in five different restaurants, losing one would hurt less. Your other investments would help balance it out.

Diversification is one of the smartest moves you can make. It protects you while still giving your money room to grow.

3. Compound Interest

This is where things get exciting. Compound interest is like a snowball rolling downhill; invested now can grow into significant wealth over time.

This is why starting today—even with just a little—matters more than waiting until you have "enough," getting bigger and bigger. Here's how it works: When your investment earns money (interest or returns), that extra money starts earning money too. Over time, this creates exponential growth.

For example, say you invest $1,000 and earn 7% per year.

Year 1: You earn $70. Your total is now $1,070.

Year 2: You earn 7% on $1,070 (not just the original $1,000). That's $75. Your total is now $1,145.

And it keeps growing from there.

The earlier you start; the more powerful compound interest becomes. Even small amounts.

Investments aren't just financial—they are spiritual. I had to ask, "Does this align with Grace?" Not just with my wallet, but with my more treasured valuables. When I was in high school, I worked at McDonald's. If I had saved just a little of each paycheck into that company's stock, I would probably be in a very different financial position. I didn't even think about it.

Understanding these three principles gives you the foundation. Now let's talk about making sure your investments match who you are.

Aligning Investments with Your Values

Think about this: every dollar you invest is like casting a vote. You're saying, "This is the kind of company—the kind of world—I want to support."

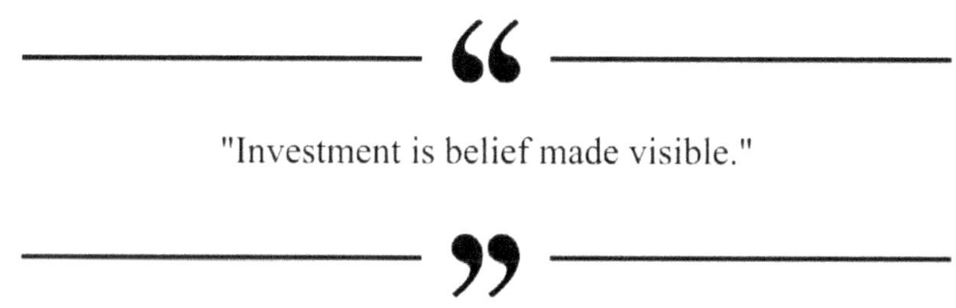

For some people, money is just money. But for those of us who take faith and values seriously, where we put our money matters. Consider ways you can invest in line with what you believe:

Sustainable Investing

Sustainable investing focuses on creating positive social and environmental impacts while also generating financial returns. It's about aligning your investments with practices that are sustainable and companies that are making a difference. Here are a few key components:

Spiritually Responsive Investing: You don't have to figure this all out alone. There are investment funds specifically designed around your values when aligned with The Grace Formula. Remember that in God's economies, Grace decided to send a Savior, to redeem the world. As people of faith, we can look to Scripture for guidance on money. God's economy is built on humility, freedom, mercy, and justice. He sent Jesus to show us this better way—and we can reflect these same mindset and values in how we invest.

Environmental, Social, and Governance (ESG) Investing. This might sound complicated, but it's simple. ESG just means looking at three things:

- **Care for the Creation:** How does this company treat the environment we live in? (Are they polluting or helping to sustain life?)
- **Social:** How do they treat people? (Are they impartial and just, without favoritism or discrimination in their labor practices? Do they return to communities?)
- **Governance:** How is the company running? (Is leadership ethical and diverse?)

Companies with strong ESG scores tend to be more responsible and often more stable over time.

Impact Investing: This is investing specifically to make a positive difference. For example, you might invest in energy companies that harvest the earth's bounty. Companies that help provide affordable housing facilities or get involved in microfinance programs that help small businesses in developing countries With impact investing, you're not just hoping to earn returns—you're actively supporting solutions to real problems.

SRI (Socially and Spiritually Responsible Investing): SRI means avoiding companies that don't match your values. For instance, if you don't want to support companies or businesses involved in harmful practices, you can invest in funds that exclude them. Many mutual funds and ETFs (exchange-traded funds) focus on SRI, making it easy to build a diversified portfolio that reflects your ethical stance.

Getting Started with Your Investment Strategy

Okay, let's make this practical. Here's a step-by-step guide to help you start investing—even if you've never done it before.

Step 1: Define Your Current State and Financial Goals

Before you invest a single dollar, ask yourself: *What do I have to invest? For what am I investing? What is my time horizon? What is my tolerance for risk? Do I have the opportunity risks figured out?*

Are you willing to consider?

- Tracking your inflows and outflows
- Recording your Financial Position and account for total, taxable, and net income
- Building an emergency savings fund?
- Just trying to build some financial margin?
- Paying off costly debt.
- Saving for retirement?
- Saving for a house down payment?
- Planning for your kids' futures?

Write down your goals. Be specific. "I want to save $10,000 in 5 years" is better than "I want to save money." Your goals will guide every decision you make. Different goals require different strategies.

Step 2: Assess Your Risk Tolerance and Time Horizon

Think about yourself with honesty:

How do you handle stress when money is involved?

If your investment dropped 15% next month, would you panic or stay calm?

When will you need this money?

There are free online quizzes that can help you figure out your risk tolerance. Or talk to a qualified financial advisor. Understanding yourself here will save you from making emotional decisions later.

Step 3: Research Sustainable Investment Options

Take time to explore investment options and opportunities that harmonize, or are in concord with, your highest values. Research spiritually responsive options, Environmental, Social and Governance (ESG) ratings, impact investing options, and socially responsible funds. Many investment platforms allow you to filter investments based on sustainability criteria. Look for funds with a track record of performance, so you know you're making sound financial choices while also supporting industries and values you believe in.

This is where you explore what's out there. Look for:

- Faith-based investment funds
- ESG funds (check their ratings and track record)
- Impact investing opportunities
- Socially and spiritually responsible mutual funds or Exchange Traded Funds (ETFs)

Many investment platforms now let you filter by values. For example, you can search for funds that avoid certain industries or focus on specific sectors like energy, technology, health care etc. It is important to look at past performance but remember—past results don't guarantee future results. Still, a fund with a solid track record is usually a safer bet than one with wild ups and downs.

Step 4: Build a Diversified Portfolio.

- Don't put all your money in one place. Spread it across different investment sectors:
- Stocks (for growth potential)
- Bonds (for stability)
- Real estate or other assets (if appropriate for your situation)

Within stocks, diversify across different industries: technology, healthcare, consumer goods, energy, manufacturing, and technology, etc. If this sounds overwhelming, consider index funds or target-date retirement funds. These automatically give you diversification. You don't have to pick individual stocks.

Step 5: Monitor and Adjust Your Portfolio

Investing isn't a set-it-and-forget-it game. Regularly review your portfolio's performance and ensure it still aligns with your goals and values. Rebalance your investments as your plan requires and as needed—this might mean selling off some assets that have grown significantly while buying more of those that may have underperformed. Many people automatically reinvest their earnings, such as dividends or other distributable outflows.

- Investing isn't "set it and forget it." You need to check in regularly to see:
- Is your portfolio still aligned with your Grace-grounded goals?
- Do you need to rebalance? (This means selling investments that haven't grown a lot and buying more of those that have, to keep your desired balance.)
- Has your life situation changed? (New job, new baby, etc.)
- Many people set a calendar reminder to review their investments once or twice a year.

The Role of Financial Advisors.

Biblical wisdom never equates victory with independence. Victory, in God's economy, is relational.

Grace invites us out of isolation and into shared discernment. When we listen humbly—welcoming wise voices, prayerful counsel, and lived experience—we step into alignment rather than striving. The absence of counsel doesn't just risk error; it quietly erodes peace.

Proverbs reminds us that guidance is a form of Grace. It is God's way of multiplying clarity, protecting our blind spots, and steadying our steps when decisions carry weight.

For leaders, stewards, and planners, this means:

- Seeking counsel is not weakness; it is wisdom practiced in community
- Victory is not speed, but alignment
- Peace is often the first sign that guidance is sufficient

When decisions are grounded in Grace, informed by wise counsel, and surrendered in prayer, the outcome may not always look dramatic—but it will be durable, fruitful, and marked by faith, hope, and love.

If this all feels like too much, that's okay. You don't have to do this alone. Consider working with a financial advisor, a broker or someone who has the expertise to help—especially one who understands faith-based or values-aligned investing. A good advisor will:

1. Help you create a personalized profile and strategy
2. Explain things in plain language and disclose how they earn.
3. Keep you accountable to your goals
4. Adjust your plan as your life changes

Look for a fiduciary advisor—someone legally required to put your interests first. Ask questions. Make sure they understand your values and aren't just trying to sell you something. Find out how broadly their planning expertise extends, how they are paid and how long they've served in this vocation to assess how trustworthy they are.

Understanding the Impact of Your Investments

Every investment you make sends a message. It supports certain companies, certain practices, and certain values.

When you invest in technology, health care, energy, or key industries that do good, you're helping build a better future. When you invest in companies with fair labor practices, you're voting for dignity in the workplace. When you choose to invest in producers of good for humanity, or even faith-aligned funds, you're stewarding your resources in a way that honors God.

On the flip side, if you invest without thinking about these things, you might unknowingly support companies that go against what you believe.

For Reflection: *Where are you currently placing your trust? Are your investments—of time, energy, and money—aligned with your values?*

You have influence here. Your investments can be part of the solution, not adding to the problem.

Three Main Takeaways

Invest with Intention: Your investment strategy should align with your values and goals. Whether you're investing for a specific purpose, retirement, or building margin for emergencies, make investment choices that reflect who you are. Sustainable and moral investing lets your money work for your future *and* make a positive impact.

Understand Risk, *Time, and Diversification*: Know your risk tolerance and time horizon. Don't put all your eggs in one basket. Balance your portfolio to protect yourself while still giving the money provided by Grace, room to grow.

Regularly Monitor and Adjust: Investing is a journey, not a one-time decision. Review your portfolio at least once or twice a year. Make sure it still matches your goals and values. Don't be afraid to make changes when needed.

Question to Ask Yourself

How can you integrate divine Grace through investments that help others, or through faith-based, sustainable, and ethical investing within your financial strategy—so your money reflects your values while building resources for the future?

As you step into the world of investing, remember this: you don't have to be perfect. You don't have to have all the answers. You just need to start where you are, with what you have, and remember that "…"*In the abundance of counselors there is victory."* (Proverbs 24:6 - Proverbs 11:14 (ESV) *"Where there is no guidance, a people falls, but in an abundance of counselors there is safety."*

Investing can feel intimidating, but it's also an opportunity. It's a way to steward what God has given you. It's a way to build a more secure future for your family. And it's a way to support the kind of world you think Grace wants to see.

You have the opportunity to shape your financial future while staying true to who you are. Take it one step at a time. Ask for help when you need it. And trust that, with wisdom and intention, your investments can be a tool for good—for yourself, for your family, and for the world around you.

Chapter 10

Returning What Grace Gives

Take a conscious moment to breathe deeply in, the Flow of Grace. I know, I know. You just finished the chapter on investing, barely figured out how to keep money, and now I want you to return it?

Here's what I want you to know: This isn't about guilt., nor is it about someone pressuring you to write bigger checks. And it's definitely not adding one more thing to your already-full plate.

This is about discovering something God built right into you: the gift of Grace's Generosity. And when you tap into it—when you let God's Grace-Flow through your decisions—something shifts. It changes not just the world around you, but inside you too.

"Generosity isn't subtraction—it's multiplication."

”

Maya hadn't slept well in months. She'd lie in bed running numbers: bills due, savings missing, retirement untouched. The math never added up to contentment or peace.

One Sunday, the priest said something that stopped her: "You can't rest your way into peace by fixing your finances first. You have to find shalom or peace first — and let it change how you manage."

Maya almost dismissed it. It sounded too simple. But that night, instead of opening her budget app, she sat quietly for ten minutes. No phone. No numbers. Just breathing and a simple prayer: *I don't have all the answers. Help me trust that I don't need them all right now.*

She didn't wake up debt-free. But she woke up lighter. And for the first time in months, she opened her budget app without dreading what she'd see.

Faith Leader Reflection: Father Nolan had seen anxiety in his own life—and in his parish. He realized that financial contentment wasn't something people arrived at after solving every problem. It was something God offered *in the middle* of the problem. Teaching that truth was one of the most radical things he'd ever done from the pulpit.

"Resting from Financial Anxiety is what the Lord's Jubilee is calling us to. Peace is a spiritual posture before it's a financial outcome.

How Can "The Grace Formula" Work in My Life?

Imagine a community where generosity flows like a river, bringing life to every dream and inspiring every heart.

Whether you're leading a family, church, school, or community organization, the 'Honor Your Heritage' approach helps you create a culture where returning isn't a burden—it's a celebration. It's about connecting with the Spirit of Grace, the one from whom all Generosity flows. When you exalt the God of Grace, life is lighter and more joyful.

Why God's Generosity Matters

Let's be upfront: being generous goes beyond money. It involves a transformed heart—a heart that's been changed by God's Grace and wants to share that with others.

Maybe right now you're thinking, "I'm barely making ends meet. I've got debt. I'm worried about the future. How am I supposed to return anything?" I hear you. And I'm not here to shame you or make you feel like you're not doing enough.

But here's what I've learned: Reflecting God's Generosity isn't about the amount. It's about the heart behind it.

I remember times of stress in life producing occasional arguments with my wife Melede about whether we could "afford" to tip 20% at a restaurant. Twenty percent! On a $30 bill! Meanwhile, I'd just spent $50 on something I can't even remember now. Our priorities get weird when we're stressed about money.

When Melede was overcome by ALS, we didn't have the time, funds, or opportunities to return and spend as we once did. Yet our provision of faith, hope, and love continued to be sufficient for each day. We were in a different spot neither of us asked for, but because of God's Grace through her and me, our returning of faith, hope, and love remained a part of our pattern.

We continued to care for each other in the cadence of repentance, forgiveness, and restoration in Grace. We continued our connection to the Alter and to the Means by which Grace-Flows. Many times, we prayed and recognized the Presence of the Holy God with us.

In the obscurity of our home, Grace's continued faithfulness sustained our hearts in Him. We were reminded that even in our darkest moments, we weren't victims or without purpose. We could still be salt and light to earth and world.

That's what God's Grace does when lives are lived in alignment with Grace that is Sufficient for the day. Grace takes what we have—no matter how small—and multiplies it. That's daily bread for sure.

Generosity: It's Already in You

This might surprise you: God didn't just command generosity. He wired it into your DNA. That is a Gift of Grace!

When you see someone struggling, what's your first instinct? To help, right? When you hear about a cause that matters, something inside you wants to be part of the solution.

That's not guilt. That's not manipulation. That's the image of God's Grace built into you—the generous Creator who gave everything for us.

The problem is that life gets complicated. Priorities follow material pursuits, Bills pile up. Stress takes over. The generous impulse planted within us gets buried under worry and fear. (And let's be honest—it also gets buried under subscriptions we forgot we signed up for.)

This chapter focuses on uncovering what's already there—creating space for God's Generosity to breathe again.

Three Truths About Returning

Before we get into the practical stuff, let's clear up some misconceptions.

1. Check Your Motives

Why do (or don't) you return (or want to return)? For people who are called by Grace, generosity flows from profound and daily gratitude for God's generous provision. We return because God gave to us first.

But let's be transparent—many times our motives get mixed up. We return out of guilt. Or obligation. Or because we want people to think well of us.

Here's the challenge: Before you return anything—whether it's money, time, or energy—ask yourself, "What is motivating me to do this?" If the answer is duty, guilt, or pressure, stop.

That's not the kind of generosity that flows from Grace. That's a burden.

True generosity comes from a grateful heart. It's an overflow, not an obligation.

If the answer is because of gratitude for Grace, continue.

2. Gratitude Changes Everything

When you shift from "I have to give" to "I get to return," everything changes. Gratitude transforms generosity from a duty into a joy.

Consider the people in your life who've been generous to you—maybe a parent, a mentor, a friend who showed up when you needed them. How did that make you feel? Grateful, right? Maybe even inspired to do likewise for others.

That's how God's generosity works. It's contagious. When you return the first fruits of your life with gratitude, you find meaning and inspire others. A ripple effect is triggered that goes way beyond your tangible allocations.

3. Vision Matters More Than Need

Here's a hard truth: people don't contribute to needs. They return the Lord's Grace to vision.

Since everyone has needs, when leaders just list problems and ask for money, it feels manipulative. But when someone casts a compelling vision—when they show you how your gift can be part of something bigger—that's when you lean in.

As a returner: You're more encouraged to return to causes that match your faith, hope, and love. Return to organizations with clear vision that matches your integrity to live it.

As a leader: Don't lead with needs. Lead with vision. Show people the impact their generosity can make. Tell true stories of transformed lives.

Beyond Check Writing: More Ways to Return

Most people think giving or contributing means cash, checks, or digital transfers. And sure, that's a well-understood way to contribute. But there's a whole menu of charitable options that might work better for your situation. How do you find out? See a charitable gift planner.

Cash and Traditional Returning

This is the most straightforward method—you return money to build the Kingdom of Grace intentionally and regularly, even periodically to causes you care about. Have you ever looked into whether your returning is done in the most effective way?

Tip: Set up automatic returning. When it happens automatically, you don't have to think about it—and you're less likely to skip it when money gets tight. This treats a top priority like a priority.

Appreciated Assets (Stocks, Real Estate)

If you own stocks or property that have increased in value, you can donate those directly to a charity.

Why it works: You avoid paying capital gains tax, and the charity gets the full value. It's a win-win.

Example: You bought stock for $1,000, and it's now worth $5,000. If you sell it and donate the cash, you'll pay taxes on that $4,000 gain. But if you donate the stock directly, you avoid the tax and get a charitable deduction for the full $5,000.

Retirement Accounts (IRAs, 401ks)

After age 72½, you're required to take minimum distributions from your IRA. But you can donate IRA assets directly from your custodian account in a rollover to charity—and it doesn't count as reportable, taxable income for the year when it is constructively received by the charitable organization. This is referred to as a Qualified Charitable Distribution or QCD and it is one of the most taxwise forms of returning under current US tax laws.

Why it works: You fulfill your distribution requirement, support a cause you care about, and reduce your taxable income. Use your previously given cash for other purposes or to reinvest.,

Donor-Advised Funds (Family Gift Fund)

Think of this as a "returning account." You contribute money to the personal gift fund (and get an immediate tax deduction), and then you decide over time which charities to support.

Why it works: It's flexible. You can contribute when you have extra cash, then distribute it over several years.

Family benefit: You can involve your kids in deciding where the money goes. It's a great way to teach the next generation about generosity.

Charitable Trusts and Gift Annuities

These are more complex, but they let you return otherwise taxable transfers into a charitable trust or charitable gift annuity, reducing capital gains shrinkage, while also securing income for yourself and/or your spouse/children.

Why it works: You support a cause you care about, receive tax benefits, and still have financial security. If your community has a Foundation or Charitable Planning entity, please ask them to partner with you to support such planning.

Who it's for: This makes sense if you're nearing retirement, facing the sale of appreciated or capital gain property, and want to return substantially without sacrificing your economic stability. It's for those with capacity to protect otherwise taxable property within a qualified trust or contract, protecting them for future income and charitable benefits.

Additionally, such charitable vehicles are extremely effective when leaving unused retirement plan assets behind. You can avoid the income tax reduction on the asset and receive income for life or a period of 20 years to children or grandchildren. At the term's end, the property becomes a gift to express your faith, while being a shrewd steward.

Heritage Habits: Blessing Generations Coming After You

Let's talk about something most people avoid: What happens to your stuff when you're gone?

I know. It's uncomfortable. But if you don't decide where your resources go, the government will decide for you. Why not use your own faith, hope and love to determine how to leave a warm glow of Grace, flowing through your decisions made during life?

Heritage Habits involves intentionally passing the flows of Grace to the next generations.

Why Heritage Matters

There's a beautiful biblical principle here: we're not just responsible for our own generation. We're called to bless the ones coming after us.

"A good person leaves an inheritance for their children's children." (Proverbs 13:22 ESV)

What if your returning could fund scholarships 50 years from now? What if the sacrifice you returned kept supporting a ministry long after you're gone? What if God's Generosity blessed grandkids, you haven't even met yet with the power and promise of Diving Grace?

Grandma Nell's Story

Let me tell you about Grandma Nell. She wasn't wealthy—she'd been a teacher her whole life, lived modestly, and saved carefully.

But she had a big heart for kids who struggled—especially those from tough backgrounds.

When Nell was 75, she wrote a letter to her grandkids explaining why education mattered to her. Then she set up a simple endowment fund. When she passed away, a portion of her estate went into that fund, and every year it provides scholarships for kids in her community.

Her grandkids still have that letter. And every year when they see another student benefit from "Grandma Nell's Scholarship," they're reminded of her reflection of God's generosity.

That's heritage. That's multiplication.

Practical Heritage Options

Here are a few ways to create a lasting impact:

Include Your Grace Values in Your Estate Plan: Designate a percentage of your estate to go to your church, a ministry, or a cause you believe in. (Pro tip: Talk to your family about this before you die.)

Name Charitable Organizations as Beneficiaries: On your retirement accounts or life insurance, you can list a charitable organization as a beneficiary. It's simple to set up and doesn't cost you anything during your lifetime.

Create a Personal Endowment or Family Gift Fund: You contribute to a fund, and the principal stays intact (endowments) where only the earnings get distributed each year, so theoretically, the fund doesn't run out. Alternatively, you may be able to spend out as determined by a designated advisor of a Donor Advised Fund or (Family Gift Fund). Either way, your gift keeps returning Grace long after you're gone.

Teach Your Kids: The best heritage isn't just money—it's values. Include your kids in conversations about returning. Let them decide where to donate. Show them why reflecting Grace's Generosity matters.

For Leaders: Creating a Culture that Reflects God's Generosity

If you're leading a church, school, or nonprofit, here's a better approach: Lead with Vision, Not Needs –Lead with God's Vision

People don't make charitable allocations to needs. They return the first fruits of their gratitude when they know they are supporting a vision that God's Grace-Flows through them. When you cast a compelling picture of what's possible, they lean in.

Instead of: "We're $20,000 short this year." Try: "Imagine a community where every kid has access to mentorship and support. Your generosity makes that possible."

Listen First, Ask Second

Before you ask anyone for anything, sit down and listen. Ask them what matters most to them, what heritage they want to leave, what they're passionate about.

When you truly listen, you'll discover how your mission connects to what's already stirring in their hearts.

Show Them the Menu

Most people think returning means cash. Educate your community. Show them the full menu of charitable 'returning' options: stocks, retirement accounts, donor-advised funds, real estate, and more.

Build Endowments to last Generations

If you want your mission to remain strong for decades, you will listen to the instruction of divine Grace and build endowments.

Steps: Be specific about what you're funding. Set transparent guidelines. Engage your community. Share the Grace.

Your Next Steps

May I encourage you to do two things?

1. Reflect

Ask yourself:

- Where is God already stirring generosity in my heart?
- What causes or organizations inspires me?
- What heritage do I want to leave?

Don't rush this. Sit with it in stillness and listen for the still small voice of Grace. Pray for it.

2. Take at Least One Action

Pick just one thing:

- Set up automatic monthly flows that return Grace to a cause you care about
- Have a conversation with your spouse or kids about reflecting God's generosity
- Write a letter to your grandkids explaining your values (like Grandma Nell)
- If you're a leader, schedule a coffee with someone in your community just to listen to this question- 'What do you believe Grace is calling you to do with the heritage you have been given when you leave it behind?
- Encourage discipled stewards to endow their annual first fruits returning to the Lord even in their death so their stewardship remains.
- Schedule a meeting with a charitable planner or advisor who represents your ministry beneficiaries to explore heritage options.

You don't have to do everything. Just do something so God's Grace doesn't go in vain.

Key Takeaways

God's Generosity Is Built Into You: God created you with a generous heart. This chapter isn't about guilting you into returning—it's about uncovering what's already there and creating space for it to flourish.

There Are Many Ways to Return: Beyond writing checks, you can return your contributions using stocks, retirement accounts, donor-advised funds, real estate, and more. Find what fits your situation and values.

Heritage Habits Matter: Your reflection and return of the Generosity of Grace can transfer the blessings to generations you'll never meet. Through heritage habits to return first-fruits to honor the God of Grace, whether its outright or in endowments, your impact can multiply long after you're gone.

Question to Ask Yourself:

How can I let God's generous Grace-Flow through my decisions—not out of obligation, but out of gratitude and contented joy?

Here's what I know: You don't have to be wealthy to reflect God's generosity. Your posture should come from a willing heart. Generosity in Grace isn't about the size of your gift. It's about the condition of your heart.

When you return from a place of Grace—when you share what you have, even if it's small—God multiplies it in ways you can't imagine.

So, start where you are. Return to the Lord of Grace cheerfully what you willingly determine is equivalent to sufficient Grace. And watch what God does with it.

Chapter 11

Trust as a Witness

Caleb's neighbor, David, had just gone through a layoff. Caleb watched from across the yard as David carried boxes to his car — calm, unhurried, almost peaceful.

Later, Caleb asked him: "How are you so calm? You just lost your job."

David shrugged. "I've been practicing trusting God with my money for years. Not perfectly. But enough that when this happened, it didn't feel like the end of the world. It felt like a season."

Caleb didn't say anything. But he watched David over the next few weeks — the way he handled the job search, the way he talked with his wife, the way he still showed up to church without a trace of bitterness. It wasn't loud. It wasn't a testimonial. But it was the most convincing thing Caleb had ever seen about what faith looked like in real life; serving through listening.

Calm stewardship speaks louder than success stories. True servant leadership emerges in compassion, not command.

Faith Leader Reflection: Pastor James had noticed something in his congregation: the people who spoke most loudly about God's provision were often the ones with the least financial stability. The quietest testimonies — the ones lived out in ordinary kitchens and ordinary decisions — were often the most powerful. He began highlighting those stories, not the dramatic ones.

As you step into a role as a leader and/or manager, it's essential to understand that leadership is more than just authority or power. It's about caring, humility, service, influence, and encouraging those around you so they flourish to be everything they were created to be. Management is more than getting it done; it's about getting it done in a quality way that represents the interests of ownership.

In this chapter, you'll explore how to embrace servant leadership or management, uncover your unique Grace promise, and lead in a way that aligns with your core values and/or within the greater mission of organizations and initiatives you support.

Uncovering Your Grace Promise

So, what does it mean to uncover your Grace promise? At its core, this concept involves recognizing the unique gifts and talents given to you that are compelling, differentiating, and true about you. This is seen in how you care. Love and serve others to reflect the image of Grace within, as salt (preservative) and light (glowing illumination). It's also seen when you are diligent in encouraging and advancing your mission so that it rings true to outsiders and insiders alike.

Reflecting on Your Journey

To start, take a moment to reflect on what drives and sharpens you. Ask yourself:

What experiences have shaped my leadership or management style? Consider the challenges you've overcome and the lessons you've learned along the way. Each setback, triumph, and moment of clarity contributes to your identity as a leader.

What strengths do I bring to my team? Identify the insight, skills, and abilities that equip you to flourish. This might be your ability to connect with others, your attention to detail, your strategic thinking, your knack for problem-solving, your diligence, or ability to think outside the box, your humility.

How Do You Uncover the Grace Promise of Your Mission?

The Mission, as a charter for living within an organization, is important for adherents or insiders. Promise is about the impact that your mission has on others/outsiders. The limitation of Mission-only planning is that it focuses on concerns of the insiders and not necessarily those externally, whom you are called to benefit. As your personal or organizational Grace promise is uncovered, it will provide a bridge to your natural vision in terms of impact on the communities you serve, both internal and external. It's what only you can do, or only you can do as well.

Effective Communication and Collaboration

Once your mission is clear, think from the 'outside-in' to uncover what your mission's impact is on those both inside and outside of your community. As a servant leader or manager, your ability to connect with your team hinges on consistency, clarity, transparency, and collaboration.

Strategies for Effective Communication

Be Consistent: Consistency is one of the most important attributes for effective communications and relations with your audiences. If the public is to interact with you, they must be able to understand what impact your mission promises to provide and then trust you.

Create Clarity and Be Transparent: Clarity helps your audiences know the impact you will have in their world. Transparency breeds trust. Share your vision, how you benefit them, your plans to deliver that benefit, and even the challenges you face or failures you've endured.

Listen Actively: Communication is a two-way street. Engaging with your team through active listening shows that you value their input and insights. If done routinely and intentionally, it strengthens relationships and creates a culture of shared aspirations and collaboration.

Share Stories: Stories are powerful tools. They resonate with people and create emotional connections. Share challenging stories that sharpened your perspectives. Share success stories and lessons within your organization to give evidence that your mission is true.

The Potency of Visioning

When you embrace strategic visioning over traditional planning, you will discover a key relational truth. As you encourage and capture people's vision of potential, and distill this down to the common ground, you will find that visioning helps you, your team, and those who are getting to know you not only obsess on immediate needs or tasks, but also allows time to consider and relate the long-term impact of your decisions.

Involve Your Team: Engage your team in visioning sessions. Encourage everyone to contribute ideas and perspectives. This collective brainstorming nurtures creativity and innovation.

Focus on the Do-able: After all of the ideas and 'visions of potential' are collected, it will be important to distill this larger vision into a vision plan that is realistic, reflects your missional key driving factors, and is achievable. In other words, your vision flows from your interpretation and application of the (100%) Grace Promise.

Emphasize Flexibility: While a vision provides direction, be open to adjusting your strategies as circumstances change. This flexibility demonstrates resilience and adaptability in your leadership and management. To do this effectively requires regular exploring, assessing, and listening.

Strategic Visioning and Accountability

As you develop your leadership, it's crucial that leaders at the top focus on the horizon, yet operate today with accountability and transparency. Developing your management requires a focus on diligence for the task at hand, while understanding the horizon.

Key Essentials of Board Leadership

Establish Clear Roles: Define the roles and responsibilities of your board members and executive staff clearly. This clarity prevents misunderstandings and ensures everyone knows their expectations and expected contributions.

Encourage Collaboration: Nurture an environment where board members collaborate and support one another. Board decisions should not cross the line of management. All staff issues should be dealt with by a top staff member or a super-volunteer team member with executive responsibilities. Executive leadership must monitor the key outcome areas for Board determinations.

Monitor Progress: Develop systems to track your organization's progress toward its key outcome metrics and goals. Remember, what you measure, you treasure.

Functioning as a Fit Fiduciary

As a servant leader on a board or in a top executive role of an organization, your fiduciary responsibility is to ensure that the resources entrusted to your organization are managed prudently, ethically, and responsibly, and that there is public trust. Here are the three top factors:

Financial Integrity: Maintain transparency in all financial dealings. Remember that trust is built in patterns, not presentations.

Resource Allocation: Make informed decisions regarding resource allocation. Prioritize investments that align with, and drive your organization's mission, identity, values, and trajectory.

Risk Management and Opportunity Cost: Identify potential risks and develop strategies and policies to guide and mitigate them. Recognize what you are giving up for every decision made.

Nurturing Stewardship Attitudes

Embodying a mindset of Grace in stewardship, which is essential for a servant leader or manager, requires recognizing that all resources—time, talent, and treasure—are ultimately entrusted to us to manage, not owned, during this lifetime.

For those who also know they are called to steward the mysteries of God, such leadership reflects the sacrificial agape love of Grace, with its undeserved mercy that is first given to us.

In any case, recognizing the source of all good things makes a difference in how goodness reigns around you.

Nurturing God's Generosity and Accountability in Grace

Model Grace's Generous Spirit: When Grace-Flows through us, we demonstrate a spirit of gratitude that compels similar action toward others and true humility in our leadership. Share your resources, time, and expertise with others, encouraging your team to adopt the same mindset that Grace gives.

Encourage Mutual Accountability and Support: Nurture a culture of mutual support and accountability by encouraging your team to take hold of the gift of repentance, moving to faithful stewarding of responsibilities. Whether you are the leader or a manager, recognize that accountability and support are always correlated. Accountability to Grace covers all.

Assess Your Impact: Regularly evaluate the impact of your stewardship efforts to ensure effectiveness. Use assessments to identify areas for improvement and celebrate successes.

Managing Key Outcome Areas

As a servant leader or manager, it's essential to identify, lead, and manage key outcomes that align with your organization's mission and vision.

Define Success: Work with your team to define what success looks like for your organization.

Develop Metrics: Establish clear metrics to evaluate the progress of each team member toward these key outcomes.

Celebrate Achievements: Take time to celebrate milestones and achievements with your team. Recognizing accomplishments boosts morale and reinforces commitment to your mission's promise. For the community of saints, the pattern of exalting the Lord will invigorate.

Motivating Accountability and Action

An effective servant leader inspires and equips their team to take up their stewardship of work, identify the source of issues, and strive for the best they were created to be.

Set Clear Expectations: Communicate your expectations regarding performance and accountability. Give each person the opportunity to relate their commitments to collective action.

Provide Support: Offer support and resources to help your team meet their goals. It requires people who can glow with the warmth of God's Grace.

Nurture a Positive Environment: Create an atmosphere where team members feel valued and appreciated.

Time Management: Your Most Precious Resource. Treat it like daily manna from Grace.

As a servant leader and a manager, effective time management is crucial. Your time is one of the most valuable resources you have.

Prioritize Tasks: Identify tasks that align most closely with your life and mission and focus your energy on these high-priority activities.

Set Boundaries: Learn to say Grace-grounded no to activities that do not align with your mission.

Delegate Effectively: Trust your team to take on responsibilities. Delegating tasks not only encourages and releases your team but also frees you to concentrate on strategic initiatives that only you must do.

The Importance of Governance

Effective leadership require a clear understanding the distinction between governance and management.

Governance involves setting the strategic direction for the organization and ensuring accountability to stakeholders within limits. Management focuses on the day-to-day operations of the organization, including implementing policies and managing resources within the limits set by the board.

As a servant leader, you must steward both governance and management responsibilities.

Embracing Your Role as a Grace Steward

As you embrace your role as a Grace Steward, remember that your journey is not solely about achieving organizational goals; it's about serving others and nurturing a culture of justice, kindness, mercy, and humbly faithful action.

Reflect on the essentials outlined in this chapter:

- What steps will you take to uncover the Grace promise of you or your mission?
- How will you communicate effectively with your team, audience, and stakeholders?
- In what ways can you model Grace in stewardship in your personal life and organization?

By committing to a servant leadership or servant management mindset, you intend to anchor decisions in Biblical stewardship, sacrifice, accountability, and strategic visioning. As such, you're

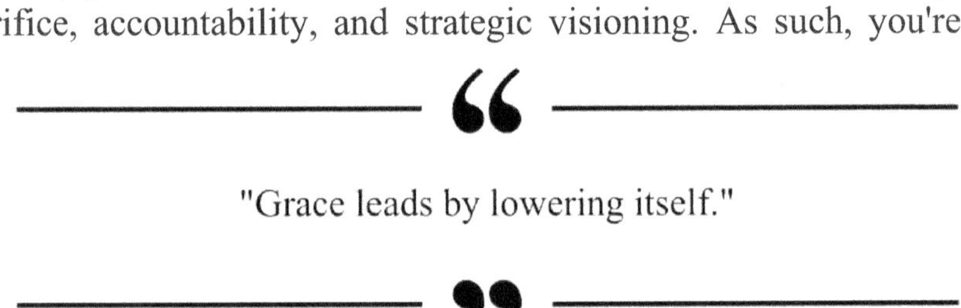

poised to make a lasting impact in your organization and community.

Three Main Takeaways

1. Uncovering Your Promise: The essence of servant leadership and servant management lies in recognizing and utilizing your unique challenges, gifts, and abilities to serve others. This self-awareness, derived from measuring how others receive the mission, enhances your effectiveness in their lives and enables you to better serve your team and community with justice, mercy, kindness, and humility.

2. Effective Communication and Collaboration: Transparent communication and collaboration create a culture of trust and engagement. By sharing your vision consistently, actively listening, and incorporating storytelling, you can inspire and motivate your team to work together towards a common goal. Remember that collaboration is a higher form of working together. The chain goes from Connection to Cooperation to Coordination to Collaboration. This is when we are better together than we are by ourselves.

3. Strategic Stewardship and Accountability Strong leadership and management demand faithful responsibility. Effective servant leaders and managers practice strategic stewardship, ensuring resources are used wisely while holding themselves and their teams accountable for growth, fulfillment, and overall success.

Stepping Into Your Grace Promise

As you conclude this chapter, we hope you have a clearer understanding of how servant leadership or management is rooted in stewardship, accountability, and vision. Such reflections of Grace transform not only organizations but also the individuals within them. By embracing servant leadership and management, you've also encouraged others to do the same, creating a ripple effect of positive impact.

Stepping fully into your Grace promise means leading with God's purpose, generosity, and authenticity. It involves putting others' needs first while also ensuring that the mission and vision of life and/or organization(s) are advanced.

This kind of leadership is not only about achieving results; it's about creating a culture where everyone faithfully flourishes to be all that they were created to be, as they feel valued, and contribute meaningfully to the greater good. *'As each has received a gift, use it to serve one another, as good stewards of God's varied Grace.'* (1 Peter 4:10 ESV)

Reflection Questions:

How will you uncover and live out your Grace promise daily?

What specific actions will you take to ensure your leadership or management aligns with your core beliefs and values?

How can you further develop your community or team, creating an environment that nurtures trust, growth, mutual accountability, encouragement and innovation?

Moving Forward as a Servant Leader or Manager

As you move forward, remember that the journey of leadership or management is ongoing. There will always be opportunities to grow, learn, and refine your approach. Continue to serve with humility, make strategic decisions with integrity, fulfill your responsibilities faithfully, and nurture your team with a spirit of mutuality, humility, and gratitude.

In the end, your success as a servant leader or a manager is measured not only by the goals you achieve, but by the positive and lasting influence you have on the people and communities served, and while serving with them.

By staying true to Grace's promise, you'll create a heritage of leadership that inspires others to embrace their own potential and to lead with purpose, just as you have done.

Your Grace Promise gives the Power to Lead and Manage

Your Grace promise is Grace's power made your power—it's what sets you apart and gives you the ability to lead with impact and meaning. Use it wisely, share it effectively, and lead with a heart full of service where Grace-Flows for the world.

Chapter 12

The Power of Stewardship Advocates

Maya was sitting across from her financial advisor for the third time this year. The numbers had improved — not dramatically, but steadily. But something else had changed too, and the coach or advocate noticed it.

"You used to come in here looking like you were bracing for bad news," he said. "Now you just look... ready." Maya smiled. "I think I stopped believing that money was something to survive. It started feeling like something to steward."

The coach nodded. "That's the shift. Everything else — the budget, the savings, the plan — that's just tools. But *that* — what you just described — that's what makes the tools work."

Maya left the meeting thinking about generosity for the first time in years. Not because she had extra. But because trust had opened a door she didn't even know was closed.

Faith Leader Reflection: Brother Justin had spent years teaching financial literacy in his parish. But he'd noticed a pattern: the congregants who grew into generous returners weren't the ones who learned the most about money. They were the ones who learned the most about *trust*. Generosity, he realized, wasn't a financial skill. It was a spiritual one — rooted in believing that God's provision was real and enough.

My role as a charitable gift planner came with a sacred responsibility and a professional expectation to listen actively to help stewards align their estate and gift planning to the objects of their bounty and love. That's when I saw the Spirit of Grace work in the hearts of stewards of Grace. Those who are called to steward the mysteries of the Gospel seek to plan their current and future intentions to bless and not to curse. Their decisions are not dependent on how large or small they manage, but grow or fall based on their faith to believe as Grace produces the Spirit's increase.

For many consumers in our culture, there is plenty of vulnerability for the average steward related to guidance in financial matters. Professional planners are ideal helpers. Not all of them have your 100% in mind, and if they can profit from their advice, this makes it all the more important to have complete trust.

Would you benefit from a network of Grace-Flow Advocates, Coaches or Facilitators, as fellow members of the City of God, who are trained to offer a confidential, listening ear and focus on what matters most to you? If you could benefit from a discerned and informed listening ear today, consider asking your community leaders to support you as you participate in the Grace Formula framework and movement.

You're navigating life, chasing your dreams, maybe still figuring out who you are and what you truly want. There's a lot to juggle—career, relationships, personal growth. (And if you're like me, you're probably dropping at least two of those balls most days.) Somewhere in there, you realize something important: you're responsible for how you manage the resources and opportunities in front of you.

This responsibility is called stewardship. It's not just about managing money or time. It's about everything placed in your care—your talents, your energy, your influence (Yes, even that pile of unread emails counts).

What if one of the best ways to grow in your decision-making and faithfulness is by seeking trustworthy coaching? Coaching that guides you to manage resources on loan from God and helps others around you flourish is the support many need to reach the reset of Jubilee.

Coaching for stewardship isn't just for executives or church leaders.

It's for you, right here, right now. It's for anyone who feels pulled to live intentionally, make better decisions, and create a positive ripple effect in their community. Let's dig into what this looks like for you.

Coaching to Encourage and Equip

Think about it: when was the last time you felt totally accepted, supported, understood, and guided in your decisions? That's what good coaching does. It's not about someone telling you what to do. It's about someone helping you uncover the answers already planted inside you. And when it comes to stewardship—how you manage your life, your resources, your future—having a trustworthy coach or mentor can be life-changing.

Imagine this: you're already doing your best to manage your money, your time, and your relationships. But you feel like something's missing (Spoiler alert: it's not more coffee, though that never hurts). That's where a Grace-Flows Coach comes in. A coach helps you see the bigger picture.

They ask the tough questions:

- Are you using your talents in a way that truly matters?
- Are you investing in the right things, the right people, the right causes?
- What is your anchor for decisions made, and how was it uncovered?

They guide you to see the Grace you've been given. Then they help you review decisions about the resources you've received—your skills, your time, your connections—and show you how to use them for a more effective alignment with Grace.

Here's the thing about coaching: it's not just about you. As you grow through the process, you'll naturally want to encourage and equip others around you to do the same. Whether it's your friends, family, or coworkers, the leadership qualities that come from being coached for stewardship will overflow into every area of your life.

Coaching for stewardship creates a cycle. When you flourish, the people around you flourish too. You can be the person who makes it known what true stewardship looks like when decisions are aligned with the 100% of Grace. Others will be inspired to seek coaching themselves.

Case Study: Jason, the Grace-Flows Coach turned economic encourager.

Jason had lived a stable life. He had the discipline and humility to live within his means and make financial decisions that reflected the Grace that gave him faith, hope, and love. Jason was a financial expert who didn't depend on a paycheck anymore. But he felt drawn to help people who couldn't afford to pay for financial advice (And let's be honest—the people who most need financial advice are usually the ones who can least afford it).

When Jason's faith community and school started teaching The Grace Formula, Jason approached the leaders with an idea. Could he work with people who needed help finding more stability in their financial choices? He wanted to represent his church's mission and offered to build a coaching ministry around Biblical truths and compassion captured in The Grace Formula.

The result? A quiet revolution.

The faith community grew in how honestly, they could talk about money (Because let's face it, most churches would rather discuss just about anything else on Sunday morning).

Now they didn't just mention money when they needed some for the building fund. They taught what the Word of God actually says about stewardship and served their neighbors in the self-sacrificial way of Grace.

Jason discovered something powerful: when you coach people through their money struggles with compassion instead of judgment, you're not just helping them balance a budget. You're helping them see how Grace shows up in every dollar, every decision, every difficult choice.

Align Stewardship with Faith

Now, let's dive deeper. Stewardship—managing blessings given by another—isn't just practical. It's spiritual too. Maybe you've grown up with faith as a central part of your life. Or maybe you've come to it more recently. Either way, coaching in stewardship helps you align your practical life with your spiritual beliefs.

What does that mean? It means seeing your time, talents, and resources as gifts entrusted to you for a reason. It means following the truth that radiates the authority in your life.

Picture this: you're sitting with your coach, talking through your goals for the next year. As you discuss your family and career plans, your coach asks you to consider how these goals line up with your faith (This is usually the moment when you realize your five-year plan might need some adjustments).

- Are you making decisions that reflect your values?
- Are you thinking about how your decisions connect to life's highest purpose?

A coach oriented in Grace-grounded decision-making will encourage you to think beyond the bottom line. They help you align your actions with something bigger—your aspirations, your faith, your sense of purpose or calling, and the impact you want to have on the world.

Stewardship in the context of Grace and Faith is about more than managing life and life's resources wisely with a heart made clean by Grace. It's about making decisions that honor the source of your values and keeping your life true and balanced. It's realizing that every opportunity, every connection, every dollar isn't just yours to use.

It's provided to you to manage with care, gratitude, and intention flowing from Grace through you to share faith, hope and love.

Consecrated Coaching helps you see these connections. It brings clarity to how your spiritual life intersects with your day-to-day decisions.

Navigate Crises with Compassion

But what about when things go wrong? Maybe you lose your job. Or there's a family crisis. Or the world feels like it's falling apart around you. (Some days it feels like all three at once, doesn't it?) Crises are where our role as stewards really gets tested. When everything is going smoothly, it's easy to feel like you've got everything under control. But during tough times? That's when decision-making really matters. And Grace-grounded coaching can make all the difference.

Imagine you're going through a rough patch, and you're not sure how to manage everything. A coach can help you navigate the crisis with compassion and without guilt—not just for others but for yourself. They'll remind you to take a step back and consider how your actions, decisions, and use of resources reflect your values, even when things are hard. Instead of reacting out of fear or frustration, coaching helps you respond with purpose and clarity.

"You don't need to be perfect to walk with someone—you just need to be present."

Crises also bring opportunities for clarity and change. Through coaching, you can learn to see challenges as moments to deepen your management of life and life's resources. You strengthen your ability to care for the people and responsibilities in your life. Whether it's financial hardship or personal struggles, stewardship coaching gives you the tools to handle crises with resilience and aligned in divine Grace.

During these tough times, coaching helps you stay afloat and expands your capacity to lead with quiet strength. And that's key. Compassionate clarity in crisis means using your resources—whether it's your time, your support network, personal and professional development, or your finances—to help build and serve others while staying grounded in the values you hold. It means becoming a steward not only for yourself, but for your faith and your community, especially when times are hard.

Three Main Takeaways

Encourage and Equip Through Coaching

Coaching helps you unlock your potential by guiding you to think deeply about how you manage your resources. It's not just about managing money, talent, or time better. It's about uncovering how you can live more intentionally and inspire others to do the same. By seeking Grace-grounded coaching, you don't just improve your own life. You create a ripple effect of encouragement and power in your mission's promise within your communities.

Align Stewardship with Faith through Grace

Faith-driven stewardship coaching helps you align your life's decisions with your spiritual values. It challenges you to consider how you can use your gifts, time, and talents to serve a greater purpose. When you make choices that honor your beliefs and recognize that everything you have is a gift that requires responsive and responsible management, you gain peace in the sufficiency of Grace.

Navigate Crises with Repentance and Compassion

Coaching equips you to handle life's inevitable crises with a contrite heart and in the compassion of God's eternal love—for others and for yourself. Instead of reacting to challenges out of fear, coaching helps you approach them with humility, confidence, clarity, and purpose. Your actions reflect your motivating values, even in difficult times. It prepares you to lead with greater consistency, resilience and care, supporting those around you while staying grounded in what truly matters.

A Question for You

How can you actively nurture a culture of encouragement in

stewardship coaching within your community that encourages and equips others while deepening your own understanding and commitment to the precepts of Grace?

Stewardship, at its core, is about recognizing the responsibility you have to manage not just what you've been given, but more importantly, who you are in the process. Whether it's seeking coaching for your own growth or creating a ripple effect by inspiring others to embrace stewardship as a calling for faithfulness, your journey starts now.

The decisions you make today—about your time, money, energy, and abilities—are shaping the future, not just for you, but for the people around you. Grace Formula Coaching can help you navigate that journey with faithfulness, purpose, clarity, and compassion.

Are you ready to take the next step?

Chapter 13

When Feelings Drive Decisions

Caleb had been offered a promotion — more money, more responsibility, more hours. On paper, it was a no-brainer. But something in his gut said *wait.*

He sat down and tried something new. Instead of just looking at the salary, he asked three questions:

Faith: Does this align with who God made me to be? *Hope:* Does this move me toward the life I believe God has for me? *Love:* Does this let me serve the people who matter most?

The salary said yes. But the hours said no to the third question — the one that mattered most. He turned down the promotion. Not out of fear. Out of clarity.

Six months later, a different opportunity appeared — one that checked all three boxes. Caleb didn't hesitate.

Faith Leader Reflection: Reverend Tom had counseled dozens of congregants facing big life decisions. He'd learned that the best financial advice wasn't financial at all. It was spiritual. Teaching people to filter decisions through Faith, Hope, and Love — the same components of the Grace Formula — gave them a compass that no spreadsheet could replace.

You probably don't realize it yet, but your emotions have been running the show for a while now (They're like that friend who always insists on picking the restaurant—except they never actually tell you where you're going).

Emotions are everywhere. They show up in that late-night anxiety about the test or assignment due tomorrow. They appear in your worry about savings. They fuel the excitement of a new opportunity. They even drive the frustration when you're trying to handle all your commitments and you're already juggling too much.

Emotions can push you toward making decisions. And they can hold you back from them too. But here's the thing: they don't just pop up randomly. Understanding them is crucial because whether you like it or not, emotions are typically influencing up to 85% of your decisions—in the economy of your life, your relationships, your identity and your future.

In this chapter, you'll figure out how to steward your emotions and how to use them to leverage control rather than letting them control you. Imagine being able to make key decisions without panic, to spend less than what you have without greed, navigate career changes with clarity, and handle relationships without letting anger or frustration dictate your actions. That's what mastering the power of emotions is all about.

So, let's break it down. By the end of this, you'll have the approach that flows from Grace, tools to take your emotions from potential wreckers to powerful drivers.

Understanding the Role of Emotions

You've probably heard people say, "Make decisions with your head, not your heart." But let's be real: emotions aren't that easy to turn off (If they were, we'd all be making perfect choices and eating way more vegetables). Whether you're aware of it or not, emotions are a massive part of how you process the world.

If you've ever felt a gut reaction to something—whether it's buying that expensive item you don't need or hesitating to apply for a job because of fear of rejection—emotions are at the heart of those decisions.

And that's not a bad thing. Emotions can help you in ways logic alone can't. For instance, hope can give you the courage to take risks that lead to new opportunities. Fear can make you cautious, keeping you from making reckless decisions. The challenge is recognizing when your emotions are steering you in a good direction—and when they're driving you toward a cliff.

Think about a time when excitement made you jump into something quickly. Maybe you bought a new car or accepted a job without thinking through the details, only to realize later that it wasn't what you wanted. Or maybe anxiety kept you from speaking up in a relationship, and later you regretted not being more honest. These are examples of how emotions can play both sides of the game. Sometimes they help. Sometimes they throw you off balance.

Case Study: Lisa's Budget and Burnout—Anxiety rooted in childhood scarcity transformed through faithful financial practices.

Lisa grew up in a household where money was tight. Really tight. Every purchase was calculated, every "yes" came with three "no's," and the message was clear: there's never enough. Sound familiar to anyone?

Fast forward to Lisa as an adult with a decent job and a stable income. You'd think the anxiety would go away, right? Wrong. She found herself working 60-hour weeks, terrified to spend money on anything beyond the basics, and constantly checking her bank account like it might disappear overnight.

The breakthrough came when Lisa started pairing faithfulness with her finances. She began naming her emotions: "I'm feeling scarcity right now, even though I have enough." She practiced gratitude for what she had instead of fixating on what might run out. And here's the key—she surrendered those old patterns to Grace.

Lisa learned that the anxiety wasn't really about money. It was about trust. Could she trust that there would be enough? Could she trust Grace to provide? When she started making financial decisions from a place of calm awareness instead of childhood panic, things changed. She still budgeted carefully, but now she could also say "yes" to things that mattered without the crushing fear.

The numbers in her bank account didn't change overnight. But her relationship with them did. And that made all the difference.

Emotional Decision-Making in Action

Let's get real for a second. Imagine you're considering a big purchase—a new laptop or maybe even a car. You're hyped, right? You start thinking about all the cool things you'll be able to do, how productive you'll be. That excitement can easily turn into an impulsive purchase (And then into buyer's remorse by Tuesday).

But what if you paused for a second and asked yourself, "Am I being logical, or is this just my excitement talking?"

On the flip side, fear can have a similar impact, just in the opposite direction. You might be too afraid to invest in a new opportunity, even though it could be great for your future. Fear can make you cling to what's safe, even when it's holding you back.

This is why understanding how emotions affect your decision-making is so useful. If you don't pay attention, you'll either be chasing every shiny object that excites you or staying stuck in the same old patterns because you're afraid of taking a leap.

Developing Emotional Intelligence

So, what's the fix? It's partly about developing something called emotional intelligence. Now, that might sound a little like pop psychology, but stay with me—it's more useful than you think.

Emotional intelligence is the ability to recognize and understand your own emotions, and also to steward them. This also develops into understanding the emotions of others.

Here's the point: emotions are not something you can just shut off. You're going to feel them, and that's good!

What you can do is become more aware of what you're feeling and why. Then, instead of reacting impulsively, you can respond thoughtfully.

The Emotional Check-In

Next time you're about to make a big decision—especially one that could affect your finances—take a beat. Literally, just stop. Close your eyes if you have to. What are you feeling? Is it excitement? Fear? Stress? Once you identify the emotion, you're halfway there.

Now ask yourself: "Is this emotion helping me make a better decision, or is it clouding my judgment?"

If it's helping you, great—ride that wave! But if it's clouding your judgment, it's time to step back and think more reasonably or logically. You're not ignoring your emotions. You're acknowledging them and then deciding whether or not they should be driving the car.

Building Your Emotional Intelligence

It's not enough just to recognize your emotions. You need to actively work on understanding how they play into your decision-making. This means taking stock of emotional systems and patterns.

Maybe you always overspend when you're stressed. Maybe you avoid difficult conversations in relationships because of fear or trauma. Start noticing these patterns and challenge yourself to learn a different response.

Building emotional intelligence doesn't happen overnight. It's like going to the gym: the more you do it, the stronger you get. And the stronger you get, the more control you have over your life. Here's a caution: At some point in time, emotion will come face to face with Grace. When that happens, and you submit your emotions to Grace, then, and only then will you find Jubilee.

Improving Decision-Making with Emotional Awareness

So now that you understand your emotions better, how do you use that understanding to make better decisions—especially when it comes to your economic and financial life? Emotions are always going to be part of the equation. So, it's not about eliminating them but integrating them in a way that benefits you and others. The way to peace includes submitting them to God's Grace.

When you're making a decision, it's easy to lean too far toward either logic or emotion. But the best decisions come when both are in balance. If you're making a financial decision, this means acknowledging your emotions—maybe you're feeling hopeful about a new investment—but also bringing in the logical side. What are the risks? What's the potential reward? In the end, the decision should be measured according to the Grace Formula which aligns and produces faith, hope and love

The Balance Between Logic and Emotion

One method you can try is creating a "decision matrix" where you list out both the logical reasons for and against a decision as well as the emotional reasons. (Yes, this might sound a little extra. But so is regretting a major decision for the next five years.)

This forces you to look at both sides clearly.

Some days I didn't feel strong. But naming emotions and surrendering them to Grace has strengthened me to withstand the onslaughts of pressure.

Emotional Regulation in Financial Decisions

Say you're feeling overwhelmed by your finances. Maybe you've got bills piling up, or you're trying to figure out how to save or invest, and it just feels like too much. That emotional overwhelm can make you react with your stressor automatic reactions, which will allow you to transfer the blame or avoid dealing with the problem altogether, which only makes it worse.

But if you've developed your emotional intelligence, you'll recognize that overwhelm as a stressor and know that you need to address it before making any decisions.

Take a step back. Do something to calm your mind—whether it's breathing, praying, listening to the Words of Grace, taking a walk, journaling, or talking it out with a friend. Then come back to the decision with a clearer head.

The Impact of Emotions on Relationships

Now let's shift gears for a minute, because emotions aren't just about how you make decisions for yourself. They also deeply affect your relationships. Whether it's your family, friends, colleagues, or romantic interests, emotions play a massive role in how you communicate and connect with others.

"Identifying (naming) emotion is the first step to releasing it."

Emotional Awareness in Conversations

Ever had a conversation with someone that spiraled into an argument? If you're married or have siblings, you don't even need to answer that. You probably weren't just discussing facts—emotions were involved. Maybe one of you felt defensive. Or maybe the other was frustrated, and things escalated.

Next time you're in a conversation that feels emotionally charged, take a moment to recognize what's going on. Ask yourself, "Am I reacting based on what they said, or am I reacting because of how I feel right now?" This small check-in can stop a lot of unnecessary arguments.

Handling Conflict with Emotional Intelligence

Conflict is inevitable in relationships. The key isn't to avoid it but to manage it in a way that strengthens your connection rather than tearing it apart. When a disagreement happens, take a step back and ask yourself: "What am I really feeling right now?" Is it anger? Hurt? Fear?

Once you can identify the emotion, you can address it directly instead of letting it control the conversation.

Recognizing the emotions of the other person is just as important. If they're upset, try to empathize with what they might be feeling. It doesn't mean you have to agree with them. But understanding where they're coming from makes it easier to find a resolution.

Emotional Regulation for Stronger Connections

Being able to regulate your emotions doesn't mean you suppress them. It means you manage them. When you're in a heated conversation, it's okay to say, "I need a minute to collect my thoughts." Taking that pause can prevent you from saying something in the heat of the moment that you'll regret later or acquiescing or backing off, and thereby avoiding the issue altogether.

Over time, stewarding emotional regulation builds trust. The people in your life will know that they can count on you to handle tough conversations with maturity and care. And that only strengthens your relationships.

Wrapping It All Up

So where does this leave you? Emotions aren't just this annoying thing you have to deal with. They're actually a powerful tool that we were given to fill our lives with joy. However, we live in a broken world. The effects of mankind's own spiritual rebellion is unmistakable, even if it is perceived in so many different ways. By understanding how emotions influence your decision-making and relationships, you can turn emotions from something that complicates your life into something that enhances it.

When you surrender your emotions to Grace—when you name them, acknowledge them, and let Grace ground your response—you move from being controlled by your feelings to being led by the Spirit of Grace and wisdom.

Key Takeaways

Emotions as Decision-Making Drivers

Your emotions influence your decisions in ways you might not even realize. Pay attention to how you feel in important moments, especially with economic and financial choices. Emotions aren't the enemy—they're information. Use them wisely.

Emotional Intelligence is a Game-Changer

Developing emotional intelligence—your ability to recognize, understand, and manage your emotions—helps you make clearer decisions and navigate life's challenges with more vitality. It's not about being emotionless. It's about being emotionally aware.

Emotions in Relationships

Your emotional state affects how you communicate with others. The more aware you are of both your own emotions and the emotions of others, the better you'll handle conflict and deepen your connections. Grace-Flows through relationships more fully when emotions are acknowledged, not suppressed.

A Question for You

How do your emotions influence your economic decisions, and what steps can you take today to better balance your logic and emotions in Grace when making big decisions?

Your emotions are a gift from God. They're not something to fear or eliminate, but they are prone to self-serving intent. Yes, emotions are part of what makes you human, what helps you connect, what drives you to care and to create. The question isn't whether you'll feel emotions—you will. The question is whether you'll let Grace guide how you respond to them.

When you learn to name your emotions, understand their source, and surrender them to Grace, you gain a power that logic alone can never provide. You become someone who makes decisions from a place of wisdom, not just reaction. You become someone who can navigate relationships with compassion, not just defensiveness.

That's the power of emotions, surrendered to Grace.

Chapter 14

Faithfulness Over Perfection

A year ago, Maya couldn't have imagined this moment. She was sitting on her back porch with a cup of coffee, watching the sun come up — and she felt *okay*. Not rich. Not debt-free. Not perfect.

But aligned.

She thought about the last twelve months: the slow, unglamorous work of facing her numbers, having hard conversations, making small choices that added up. She thought about the mornings she prayed before opening her budget. The evenings she called her sister instead of stewing alone.

None of it had been dramatic. All of it had been real.

She opened her journal and wrote something she'd never written before: *I'm not trying to earn my life anymore. I'm living it.*

That, she realized, was what the 100% Life actually felt like. Not a destination. A way of walking.

Faith Leader Reflection: Deaconess Anna had spent twenty years in ministry. She'd seen people come to faith through big moments — worship, crises, miracles. But the deepest, most lasting transformations she'd witnessed were quiet ones. People who slowly, day by day, let Grace into every part of their lives — including the parts no one else could see. The 100% Life wasn't a headline. It was a heartbeat.

Tiny decisions stacked like bricks. Faithfulness in small things created peace.

Time has a way of slipping through your fingers. (One minute you're figuring out your first paycheck, the next you're wondering where the last decade went.) As you contemplate your future, mastering financial discipline becomes more than just a goal—it's a necessity. It's not merely about accumulating wealth. It's about being faithful to your highest values and crafting a secure and fulfilling life going forward.

Your focus has shifted. It's no longer just about what you can earn. It's about how well you manage and protect what you have. You've likely seen friends and family grapple with their own financial challenges, gaining unique perspectives from their experiences. This knowledge gives you power to make wiser choices that align with your faith, your values, and your long-term objectives.

Anchor Financial Discipline to Your Values

Financial discipline is baked into a lifestyle—a commitment to making deliberate choices that promote stability, generosity, and growth. You know that financial freedom doesn't come from a windfall or an inheritance. It's built over time through conscious efforts, habits, and decisions.

The Power of Small Choices

You may not have thought much about the little decisions in your life, but they have a monumental impact on your financial health. Each choice, no matter how small, ripples out and builds up over time. Think back to when impulse buys were regular occurrences—splurging on the latest smartphone or eating out more than you should have, hardly realizing how these choices drained your wallet (And let's not even talk about those subscriptions you forgot to cancel).

Now you approach spending with a more discerning eye. Each time you choose a homemade meal over dining out or skip buying that trendy gadget, you reinforce your commitment to discipline. These small choices contribute to your overall financial well-being.

Consider tracking your spending with a list, spreadsheet, journal software or app. This helps you identify patterns that lead to unnecessary expenses. Ask yourself, "What choices can I make today that will benefit my, and my loved ones' future?"

Creating a Realistic Spending Plan

Creating a spending plan that fits your lifestyle is both a science and an art. Your budget should reflect not just income versus expenses, but also your values and goals. Start by assessing your income and fixed expenses—housing, utilities, insurance. Next, evaluate variable expenses—groceries, transportation, entertainment. Create categories that resonate with your life. Your spending plan or budget becomes a roadmap, guiding you toward a balanced financial life. BTW- Do you see returning to Grace to reflect Grace as a fixed or variable expense? This question begins to separate those who understand their alignment and those who don't.

Don't forget about savings. Establish a monthly savings goal that aligns with your retirement plans and future aspirations. By prioritizing savings, you create a financial margin that provides funds and peace of mind when uncertainties arise.

Debt Management

Reflecting on lingering debt is necessary hard work. Mastering financial discipline requires managing debt wisely as part of your overall plan. Debt can help you build wealth, but if left unchecked, it can also hinder your progress and obligate your future.

Evaluate your current debt situation. Are you comfortable with your debt-to-income ratio? If you're carrying high-interest debt, create a strategy for repayment. Prioritize paying off high-interest debts first. Consider using the debt snowball or avalanche methods to accelerate your repayment efforts. We plan to provide such a tool at www.Graceflows.org.

At the same time, leverage debt strategically. A low-interest mortgage can be an asset, especially if your investments yield higher returns. Avoid taking on new debt for non-essential purchases. (Your future self will thank you for saying no to that impulse boat or purchase.)

Emergency Savings

You've heard countless stories of individuals facing unexpected expenses—medical emergencies, car repairs, job loss. The stress that follows when there's no financial cushion is real. I know. When our son Micah was in his second year, he was diagnosed with a Medulloblastoma tumor on his brainstem. We experienced such financial turbulence but Grace gave us hope.

Aim to build an emergency savings fund covering three to six months of living expenses. This safety net gives you peace of mind. Keep these funds in a separate savings account to avoid temptation. If you have to convince yourself it's an emergency, it's probably not.

Once your emergency fund reaches a comfortable level, consider other financial goals like contributing to retirement or saving for significant purchases or long-term stability.

Darius and the 90-Day Scripture Journey

Darius was drowning—not in water, but in debt, decisions, and constant anxiety. He had a decent job, but somehow the money always disappeared before the month did. Credit cards were maxed. The savings account was a joke. The stress affected everything—his sleep, his relationships, his faith.

Then someone mentioned a 90-Day Scripture Challenge focused on biblical financial principles. Darius almost didn't sign up. Another program? Another thing to fail at? But something nudged him. Maybe it was Grace.

The challenge was simple: read a different Scripture passage about stewardship each day for 90 days. But each reading came with a tiny, practical action step. Day 1: practice gratitude. Day 15: list all your debts. Day 30: pick one debt to attack first.

Darius started noticing patterns. The Scriptures weren't just telling him to "try harder." They were showing him that God cares about the practical, everyday details of his financial life. That Grace wasn't just for Sunday morning—it was for Tuesday's budget meeting with himself.

By Day 45, something shifted. Darius wasn't just reading Scripture—he was letting it reshape how he thought about money. He started tracking expenses (those daily coffee runs added up to a car payment). He created his first real budget with the help of an advocate and coach, and stuck to it. He set up automatic savings transfers before he could spend the money.

The breakthrough came around Day 60. Darius realized that financial discipline wasn't about restriction—it was about freedom. Every dollar he managed wisely was a vote for the life he actually wanted. And when he stumbled (because he did, several times), Grace was there. Not guilt. Grace.

By Day 90, Darius had paid off two credit cards and built a small emergency savings fund. But more importantly, his whole relationship with money had changed. When Scripture and financial practice work together, when Grace guides your decisions instead of fear or shame, real transformation happens.

Building Your Financial Future

Investing with Intention: Your investment strategy should reflect both your current situation and long-term goals. Diversification protects your investments while allowing for growth. If you're not an expert at picking individual securities, mutual funds make it easier to choose options that fit your situation and risk tolerance. Consider consulting with a qualified advisor who can provide tailored guidance.

Health Care Costs: As you age, health care costs become increasingly important. Assess your insurance coverage and plan for future medical expenses. Investigate long-term care insurance options. Consider setting up a Health Savings Account (HSA) if you have a high-deductible health plan for tax-free savings on medical expenses.

Financial Literacy: Financial literacy is a lifelong journey. Take time to educate yourself on how money works and how you work money. You can learn about savings and investment strategies, retirement planning, and tax implications. Read books, attend workshops, take online courses. Surround yourself with financially savvy and Grace aligned individuals who can share their experiences.

Setting Goals: Define clear financial goals. Whether it's becoming debt-free, returning as you want, traveling, buying a home, or enjoying a well-funded retirement, having specific goals gives you something to strive for. Break goals into short-term, medium-term, and long-term categories. Review and adjust them regularly as life circumstances change.

Finding Contentment and Resilience

Financial discipline isn't solely about restriction. It's really about finding joy and freedom in your choices. Strike a balance between returning to proclaim faith, saving for the future, and enjoying the present. Allocate a portion of your budget for charitable returning, especially returning that honors the Heritage of Grace, travel, hobbies, or quality time with loved ones. This balance leads to a fulfilling life, rich in experiences and memories. Sufficiency replaces scarcity.

Life is unpredictable. Nurturing patterns that support resilience allows you to adapt to changes while continuing your financial journey. Every setback is an opportunity for growth. Your experiences have shaped you, and you're well-prepared to face whatever comes next.

"Discipline is choosing what matters most—again and again."

Mastering financial discipline is not just about numbers. Grace invites you to create a life you love. You have the tools and wisdom to make informed choices that align with your deepest held values and goals. With each step, you're not just managing money—you're crafting a heritage for your loved ones.

The choices you make today will shape the life you lead tomorrow. Let Grace guide your decision-making.

Key Takeaways

Small Choices Build Patterns of Discipline: Financial discipline is built through everyday decisions. Small, mindful choices significantly impact your overall well-being.

Budget Reflects Your Values: Your budget should include all income and expenses and reflect your values and goals, creating a roadmap for your spending.

Manage Debt Wisely: Balance the benefits of leveraging low-interest debt against the risks of high-interest balances to maintain financial freedom. Put your payment of each debt on a multi-year plan and notice how debt captivates your future.

Build Emergency Security: An emergency fund covering three to six months of expenses creates a peace of mind cushion for life's uncertainties.

Invest with Purpose: Align your savings and investment strategy with your risk tolerance and long-term goals, reviewing and adjusting periodically. Learn to be aware of what you give up for decisions made.

Plan for Health Costs: Assess insurance coverage and consider long-term care options to prepare for potential medical expenses.

Commit to Learning: Continuous education enhances your financial understanding, providing clarity for informed decisions.

Set Clear Goals: Define specific, actionable financial goals broken into short, medium, and long-term categories to stay focused and accountable.

Balance Returning, Saving and Living: Strike a balance between allocating charitable returns outside of your home or interests, saving for the future and enjoying life today through returning and meaningful experiences. Learn to be content with the sufficiency of Grace.

Embrace Resilience: Life is unpredictable. Nurturing resilience allows you to adapt to changes while continuing your financial journey.

The 100% Life

Grace (100%) = Faith (__%) + Hope (__%) + Love (___%).

A Question for You

What small choice will you commit to making today that could positively impact your future? If you can't describe them, ask for someone with compassion to help.

Financial discipline isn't about perfection. It's about faithfulness. It's about showing up, day after day, and making the small choices that stack like bricks into something solid and secure. And when you stumble—because you will—Grace is there to lift you up and remind you that tomorrow is a new day to choose wisely again.

You don't have to have all the answers. You just have to be willing to learn, to grow, and to let Grace guide your steps. That's where true financial freedom begins.

Chapter 15

Grace When the Money Runs Out

The layoff came on a Tuesday. Caleb sat in the HR office, nodded, shook hands, and walked to his car. He sat there for a long time.

A year ago, this would have been the end of the world. The shame. The panic. The spiral of "what if" that kept him up until 3 AM.

But something had changed. He thought about the small acts of trust he'd been practicing—the penitent pauses, the prayers, the conversations. He thought about David next door, calm in his own storm. He thought about the formula he'd been living: Faith in God's plan. Hope for what was coming. Love for the people who needed him to stay steady.

He didn't have answers. He didn't have a backup plan. But he had something he hadn't had before: an anchor and foundation that didn't crack when the ground shifted.

He drove home. Told his wife. And together, they made a plan—not out of fear, but out of trust.

Faith Leader Reflection: Pastor Miguel had seen congregants destroyed by financial hardship—and he'd seen others walk through it with Grace intact. The difference was never the size of the problem. It was the size of the foundation underneath and the anchor your life is attached to. His job, he realized, wasn't to prevent storms. It was to help his people build something sturdy enough to stand on when they came.

Addressing Financial Challenges with Grace and Resilience

Take a deep breath. You're about to walk through one of life's trickiest landscapes—the financial terrain filled with obstacles that sometimes feel bigger than your faith, your budget, and your sanity combined.

But here's what I've learned across four decades of ministry related service and three generations of missionary heritage: facing financial challenges isn't just a test of your spreadsheet skills. It's a test of your character, your resilience, and whether you really believe that Grace-Flows even when the bank account doesn't.

By the end of this chapter, you won't just understand practical steps (though we'll cover those). You'll hopefully embrace a mindset that transforms financial pressure into spiritual growth. That's the Grace Formula at work: Grace (100%) = Faith (10%) + Hope (10%) + Love (80%).

> Grace doesn't remove the storm — it changes how you walk through it.

”

The Reality Check We All Need

Let's get real: financial challenges are the great equalizer. Pastor or plumber, missionary kid or millionaire—everyone faces money troubles at some point. This reality is an outcome of our disharmonious life and world.

You know that feeling. Bills stacking up like Jenga blocks. The unexpected car repair that arrives the same week as the medical bill. The promotion that didn't happen right when you needed it most. The savings account that looks more like a rounding error than an emergency fund.

Here's the liberating truth: you're not defined by your bank balance. You're defined by how Grace formed you to respond when life sends you the invoice.

We hit walls. But Grace met us there. Each obstacle became holy ground.

The question isn't *if* you'll face financial challenges. It's *how* you'll respond when they show up.

Shift Your Mindset (Because Panic Isn't a Strategy)

Remember those moments when financial stress felt like a tidal wave? When you canceled plans, cut back on coffee, or faced the tough decision to move, change jobs, or delay a big purchase?

Each of those experiences—as painful as they were—forged resilience you didn't know you had.

Here's the shift: stop viewing obstacles as setbacks. Start seeing them as a setup for growth. (Yes, I know that sounds like a motivational poster. But it's also true.)

Set realistic goals and break them into bite-sized pieces. If you're tackling debt, don't try to eat the entire elephant in one sitting. (Also, don't eat elephants. They're endangered and taste terrible.)

Instead, identify what you can realistically accomplish each month. Each payment becomes a victory. Each small win builds momentum toward your bigger goal.

Get Brutally Honest About Where You Stand

You can't navigate out of a mess you won't acknowledge. So, grab a notebook, pour some coffee or a favorite beverage, and dive into your financial reality.

List every income source—salary, side gigs, investments, that mysterious $20 that keeps appearing in your coat pocket. Then break down your monthly expenses: essentials (rent, utilities, groceries) and discretionary (dining out, subscriptions, impulse Amazon purchases at 2 AM).

This assessment reveals where your money actually goes versus where you *think* it goes. You might discover subscriptions you forgot existed. (Looking at you, a premium app from 2019 that charges $9.99 monthly for features you never use.)

Awareness is the first step from financial chaos to financial clarity. Map out your spending patterns and you'll be equipped to make informed decisions instead of reactive ones.

Build Your Emergency Fund (Even If It Starts Small)

Life is unpredictable. Having an emergency fund is like having financial shock absorbers—it cushions the blow when life hits a pothole.

Conventional wisdom says save three to six months of living expenses. If that feels overwhelming (and it should—that's a big number), start small. Really small. Even $10 or $25 per month.

Automate it. Set up a transfer from checking to savings each month. Watch those small contributions accumulate into a robust safety net.

Think of your emergency savings fund as financial insurance. When it exists, you stop living in constant "what if" mode and start living in "I'm prepared" mode. That shift alone is worth the discipline.

You Don't Have to Do This Alone

Here's permission you didn't know you needed: seek professional guidance.

(Proverbs 15:22 ESV) says it plainly: "Plans fail for lack of counsel, but with many advisers they succeed." That's not just ancient wisdom—it's also really good advice for contemporary planning.

A qualified financial advisor can assess your unique situation, create a personalized plan, and provide accountability as you work toward your goals. Be transparent. The more honest you are about your financial reality, the better guidance you'll receive.

Also explore community resources offering free or low-cost

financial education. Many organizations provide workshops focused on financial literacy, helping you build confidence in managing life's resources as a steward of Grace.

Tackle Debt Strategically

If debt feels like a weight pressing down on you, it's time for a strategic approach.

List all your debts, categorizing them by interest rates and payment terms. High-interest debt should be your priority—it's costing you the most.

Consider two proven methods:

The Snowball Method: Pay off your smallest debts first while making minimum payments on larger ones. Each paid-off debt feels like a victory, building psychological momentum. Turns out, finance is partly math and partly therapy.

The Avalanche Method: Prioritize high-interest debts to save money on interest over time. It's more mathematically efficient, even if it's less immediately gratifying.

Whichever method you choose, create a structured repayment plan. Outline monthly payments and set a timeline for becoming debt-free. Then celebrate each milestone—because progress deserves recognition.

"Grace doesn't remove hardship—it repurposes it."

Embrace Frugality Without Losing Joy

Navigating financial challenges may require lifestyle adjustments.

But here's what frugal doesn't mean: joyless, boring, or deprived. Frugal means making conscious choices aligned with your values. It means distinguishing between what brings genuine happiness and what just provides the facade or a mirage of it.

Evaluate your discretionary spending. Unused subscriptions? Dining habits that could use adjustment? Credit card fees that aren't benefiting you?

Cook at home more often. Bonus: you'll discover you're either a surprisingly good cook or hilariously bad at it. Either way, it's cheaper entertainment than streaming services.

Explore alternative entertainment: community events, outdoor activities, DIY projects. Simple pleasures often provide deeper satisfaction than expensive ones—and they redirect funds toward your actual goals.

Build Multiple Income Streams

In today's economy, diversifying income isn't just smart—it's essential.

Consider your skills and passions. Got a hobby that could generate income? Expertise that translates into income opportunities? Side projects boost income while letting you pursue interests meaningfully.

Investing can also build wealth over time. Educate yourself about options—stocks, bonds, real estate, mutual funds. Create a diversified portfolio aligned with your risk tolerance and long-term objectives.

(Disclaimer: This message is coming from a Grace interpreter, not a financial planner. So, while I can encourage investment, don't ask me to pick your stocks. My track record involves faith, not futures trading.)

Develop Your Long-Term Financial Plan

Your long-term plan is your roadmap through financial fog.

Outline goals in three categories:

- Short-term: Emergency savings fund, debt reduction
- Medium-term: Saving for a home, education, major purchase
- Long-term: Retirement planning, leaving a heritage for family, community, or ministry

Create a detailed action plan with timelines and resource allocation. Review and adjust regularly as circumstances change.

Your plan isn't set in stone—it's written in pencil with a good eraser.

Nurture Your Support System

Financial challenges feel overwhelming when you face them alone. Build a support system that provides encouragement and accountability.

Surround yourself with family, friends, or peers who understand your goals. Consider joining (or forming) a financial support group where members share experiences and strategies in an environment of Grace, not guilt.

Find an accountability partner—someone committed to improving their financial situation. Regular check-ins keep you on track while creating space to share sorrows and celebrate successes together.

Community transforms lonely struggle into shared journey.

Practice Mindfulness in Financial Decision-Making

Financial challenges trigger strong emotions: stress, anxiety, fear, occasional panic buying at Target.

Mindfulness helps you step back and make decisions with clarity instead of reactivity.

Before you make significant financial decisions, pause and breathe. Reflect on whether this choice aligns with your faith, values, and goals. Avoid impulsive decisions driven by fear or external pressure.

Incorporate mindfulness practices—prayer, meditation, Scripture reading, receiving the ways in which Grace is imparted to us, journaling—to develop awareness of your financial emotions and patterns. When you understand your triggers, you make better decisions aligned with your long-term vision.

Embracing Resilience and Growth

As you navigate financial challenges, remember: resilience is your Grace weapon.

Embrace lessons learned from past experiences. Let them guide you toward a brighter future. By developing resilience, assessing your situation honestly, building emergency savings, seeking wise counsel, prioritizing debt repayment, and nurturing community, you're equipped not just to survive but to flourish.

Your worldview shapes how you approach money and resources. Embrace each challenge as an opportunity. Practice gratitude for progress along the way.

Your journey is unique, filled with ups and downs. But with each step, you're closer to the financial freedom and stability you desire.

You are not alone. Be confident! Grace covers you.

Your Next Steps

Reflect: Write down your current financial challenges. What steps can you take today—not tomorrow, not next week—to address them?

Plan: Create a financial roadmap outlining short-term and long-term goals. What milestones will you set?

Connect: Reach out to a financial advisor or trusted friend to discuss your situation. Remember Proverbs 15:22—many advisers ensure success.

Practice Mindfulness: Set aside weekly time to review your financial decisions. How do they align with your faith, values, and goals?

Each small step counts. Each decision matters. Each moment of awareness moves you forward.

Question for Reflection: What financial challenge have you faced that ultimately led to personal growth? How can you apply that experience to your current situation?

Journey-Meditations resources: Visualize your current challenges bathed in light. What shifts when you imagine them through Grace? You may find more encouragement in a curated journey through the Economies of Grace for you. You can learn more in the last section of this book.

Chapter 16

Getting Back on Your Feet

Five years into marriage, Melede and I were building what we thought was a solid foundation. We worked hard. Paid our bills. Raised our daughter Rachel. We were doing what young families do—putting one foot in front of the other, trusting God with each step.

When our son Micah was born, I did what I'd done when Rachel arrived. I went to the Lord's House to thank God for this gift. I asked the Lord of Grace, in faith, to prosper the work of our hands.

Then came that Friday afternoon at Dr. Nelson's office.

We thought it was a routine checkup. Instead, the doctor told us Micah had a tumor the size of a golf ball on his brainstem. Surgery was scheduled for Tuesday morning. We needed to have him at the hospital by Monday.

The anxiety hit like a fist to the chest. Our bodies shook. Our emotions went wild. This was life or death for our son.

And here's what made it even harder: Just weeks before, I'd made a financial decision that was now daunting to me. When I took my first calling as a teacher and minister of the Gospel, a professional advisor had encouraged me to opt out of Social Security. "You'll do better investing in mutual funds," he said. So, I did.

But something didn't sit right. Eight years later, when I realized I didn't understand what I'd done fully, I reversed course and jumped back in to the system. That reversal created a multi-thousand-dollar expense—right before we got Micah's diagnosis.

I could feel the walls closing in. I've always had a fairly high tolerance for risk, but this? This was a crisis that would cost more than I could pay.

In the parking lot, Melede and I stood between our two cars, trying to process what we'd just heard. We needed to drive home separately—we'd come from different places—but neither of us wanted to be alone with our thoughts.

That's when the Spirit of Grace came to us in a most marvelous way.

I looked at Melede and said, "Micah belongs to the Lord. God will do what He wants with him. His Grace will be enough for us as we go through this."

We prayed right there in the parking lot. We asked God, in His Grace and Mercy, to send the Holy Angels to be with us and protect our son and us in all our ways.

And then something happened. A calm peace descended on both our hearts. Not because our circumstances changed—they hadn't. But because we remembered whose hands, we were in.

Over the next five years, we lived under tight financial conditions. Really tight. We had our home, and we were grateful for that. But the medical bills seemed endless. Every month, another payment. Every month, wondering if we'd have enough. Managing cash flow seemed to be a big dark sea, full of mines.

But every day, we thanked God for the blessings of love, hope and faith, and health insurance. We saw it as evidence of Grace meeting us in our need.

It wasn't easy. It wasn't pretty. But we moved forward one decision at a time, always grounding those decisions in the infinite kindness of divine Grace.

Micah survived his fight with Medulloblastoma. He carries scars from that battle—physical and emotional. But today, he lives a beautiful life, loving those around him with the Love he has received from Grace.

Rachel has grown into a woman with a loving spouse and a beautiful family of her own. They're all growing in Grace, each day.

We rebuilt—financially, emotionally, spiritually.

Grace was our mortar.

Let's be truthful. Life doesn't always go according to plan.

Maybe you're in debt up to your ears. Perhaps you just got laid off from a job you loved. Maybe unexpected medical bills wiped out your savings. Or maybe your car broke down, and the repair costs more than the car is worth. When money problems hit, they rarely come alone. They pile up like uninvited guests at your door.

Here's what I want you to know: This doesn't define you. It doesn't mean you failed. It just means you're human, living in a world where things break, people lose jobs, and life throws curveballs.

I've been there. My family has been there. And we rebuilt—not just financially, but emotionally and spiritually too. Grace was our mortar, holding everything together when our own strength ran out.

This chapter is about what to do when you're in the thick of it. Not someday. Right now.

Step 1: Take a Deep Breath and Look at the Numbers

I know it's scary. Looking at your bank account when you know it's bad feels like opening a door you'd rather keep closed. But avoiding it won't make it better.

Here's what you need to know and do:

Recognize that this reality is an opportunity for you to cast off the old self which has been too bent on doing your own thing in your own ways, and accept with gratitude how your very existence is a gift given to you by God's Grace in Jesus, the Christ. In this mindset, forgiveness provides the reset that can change your attitudes and motivations.

Gather your facts. Pull out everything—bank statements, bills, pay stubs, and credit card statements. Everything. Don't hide from any of it.

Write down what's coming in. List every dollar you have coming in each month. Your paycheck, unemployment benefits, side gig money—all of it.

Write down what's going out. Every single expense. Rent, groceries, utilities, car payment, Netflix, coffee runs—everything.

Do the math. Income minus expenses equals your cash flow. If the number is negative, don't panic. You're not alone, and you can fix this.

Remember in hope that the emotional ark that you are likely to go through when you apply the Grace Formula will look like this:

Joy → Crisis → Desperation → Peace → Perseverance → Restoration

Step 2: Sort Your Expenses

Now that you know where your money goes, it's time to make some tough choices. Split your expenses into two piles:

Must-Haves (Essentials):

- Return first-fruits
- Rent or mortgage
- Groceries (not eating out—actual groceries)
- Utilities (water, electricity, heat)
- Transportation to work
- Basic phone service
- Minimum debt payments

Nice to Have (Non-Essentials):

- Streaming services

- Eating out
- Shopping for fun
- Gym memberships
- Premium anything

For the next few months, you're going to focus only on the must-haves. Everything else? Put it on pause.

I know it's hard. But this is temporary. You're climbing out of a hole, and every dollar you save is another step up. What you don't want to continue to do is try to find other's money to shackle you again.

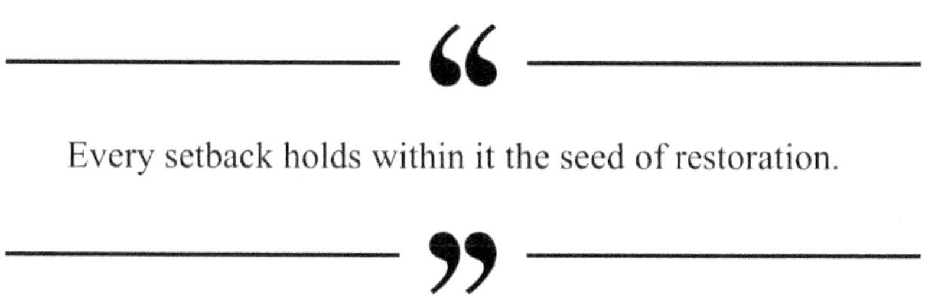

Step 3: Make Your Comeback Plan

Now you know where you stand. Time to make a plan to get back on solid ground.

Rank your bills by urgency. What absolutely must get paid this week? What happens if you miss that payment? Will they shut off your power? Will you lose your car? Start with the most urgent.

Create a barebones budget. Take your must-have list and create a spending plan for the next month. This isn't forever. This is your survival budget while you recover.

Set one small goal. Maybe it's saving $50 this month. Maybe it's paying off one small bill. Pick something you can actually achieve. Small wins build momentum.

Step 4: Find Extra Money (Yes, You Can)

When you're in crisis mode, getting creative about income isn't optional. Here are some real ways people have brought in extra cash:

Use what you already know. Can you write? Design? Fix things? Code? Build? Cook? Platforms like Upwork, Fiverr, or TaskRabbit can connect you with people who need your skills.

Offer services in your neighborhood. Dog walking. Babysitting. Lawn care. House cleaning. Snow shoveling. These aren't glamorous, but they're honest work that pays.

Sell stuff you don't need. Look around your home. What are you not using? Facebook Marketplace, Craigslist, or a garage sale can turn clutter into cash.

Take a temporary job. Retail stores, restaurants, delivery services—they often hire quickly. Even 15-20 hours a week can make a real difference while you're getting back on your feet.

The key? Pick something and start. Action beats anxiety every time.

Step 5: Talk to the People You Owe Money To

This is the part most people avoid. But here's the truth: Your creditors would rather work with you than never hear from you at all. Call them before they call you. Explain what happened. Be honest. "I lost my job." "I had a medical emergency." "I'm trying to figure this out."

Ask what they can do. Many companies have hardship programs. They might:

- Let you skip a payment or two
- Lower your interest rate temporarily
- Set up a payment plan you can actually afford

Get everything in writing. If they agree to help, ask them to email or mail you the details. Keep records of every conversation.

Step 6: Celebrate the Small Stuff

This part matters more than you might think.

When you're stressed about money, it's easy to only see what's going wrong. But you need to notice what's going right, too.

Did you stick to your budget this week? That's worth celebrating. Did you make $50 from a side gig? That's progress. Did you avoid spending money on something you didn't need? You're building new habits.

Write down your wins. Tell someone you trust. Acknowledge that you're moving forward, even if it's slower than you'd like.

The Truth About Setbacks

Here's what I've learned from my own financial struggles and from watching others navigate theirs:

Every setback is also a setup for a comeback.

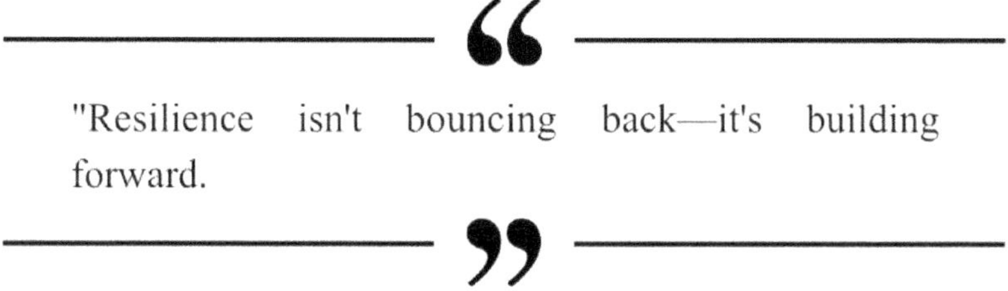

You're not just rebuilding your bank account. You're building resilience. You're learning what really matters. You're discovering strength you didn't know you had.

Grace meets us in these moments. Not when we have it all together, but when we're honest about where we are and willing to take the next step.

Your 30-Day Action Plan

<u>Week 1</u>:

- Gather all your financial information

- Calculate your cash flow (inflows minus outflows)
- Identify must-have vs. nice-to-have expenses

Week 2:

- Create your survival plan or budget
- Contact creditors if needed
- Research one income opportunity

Week 3:

- Start your income opportunity
- Stick to your spending plan or budget
- Celebrate one small win

Week 4:

- Review what's working
- Adjust what's not
- Set your goal for next month

Remember: You're not climbing out of this hole overnight. But you are climbing.

And every step-up, counts!

Key Takeaways

Face it head-on. Avoiding your financial situation won't make it better. Gather the facts, do the math, and see where you really stand.

Focus on essentials. Cut everything that isn't necessary for survival. This is temporary. You can add things back later.

Get creative with income. Use your skills, offer services, and take temporary work. Every dollar you earn is another step toward stability.

Talk to creditors. They'd rather work with you than lose you completely. Ask for help.

Celebrate progress. Small wins matter. Notice them. Acknowledge them. They're proof you're moving forward.

For Reflection

Think about a time when you faced a financial challenge and came through it. What did you learn about yourself? What strategy worked that you could use again?

What's one action you can take this week to start moving toward financial stability? How can you apply the Grace Formula to help?

We rebuilt, not just financially, but spiritually. Every recovery taught me resilience shaped by Grace.

Chapter 17

Grace Gives You Enough

In the last chapter, we talked about what to do when money gets tight right now. This chapter? This is about making sure you're ready for whatever comes next.

Think of it like this: Chapter 16 was the emergency room. This chapter is preventive medicine.

You can't control everything that happens in life. But you can control how you anchor yourself and how prepared you are when it does.

Right in the middle of Micah's cancer treatment—after his surgery, while we were still figuring out how to breathe again—our second daughter, Christa, was born.

Like all our children, she had a blood compatibility issue that needed careful monitoring. It stemmed from an oversight when our first daughter, Rachel, was born. So, the doctors knew to watch Christa's bilirubin levels for jaundice closely after birth.

But this was a teaching hospital. Extremely busy. And in the chaos, someone made a mistake. They discharged Christa without the follow-up blood work nor lights to treat her. That night, her bilirubin spiked to over 21, a highly-dangerous level.

We had to rush her back to the emergency room. Our newborn daughter needed a complete blood transfusion to save her life.

We prayed. We asked God to preserve her life. And that prayer was answered in spades. That little girl grew up to become a teacher, a wife, a mother of four beautiful children, and a woman who walks in Grace.

The emotional tension from that experience? It was infuriating. But it didn't overcome us. We cast our cares upon the Lord of Grace, whose desire for us is always best and for our good. In time, I repented for my anger, which wasn't a helpful factor except to allow me to release pressure.

And then Grace gave us more.

Our fourth child, Matthew, was born a year later. He brought his mom, Melede, a joy we could never have expected—joy we didn't even know we wanted. Looking back, we didn't know what to expect from any of it. Medical trouble surrounded our family on every side. Medical crises. Financial strain. The constant weight of uncertainty.

But Grace gave us more.

More children to love. More reasons to trust. More evidence that we weren't alone.

As we recognized all the ministering spirits who had been sent to help us—medical professionals, friends, family, and even our own children—we discovered something: We had sufficiency. Not scarcity. Not easy. But enough.

And with that sufficiency, we could move forward. Not in fear, but in the wisdom that Grace gives. That's what this chapter is about. Preparation isn't about fear—it's about growing in wisdom.

Understanding Money Seasons

The economy has seasons, just like the weather. Sometimes things are growing and sunny. Sometimes there's a storm. Neither lasts forever.

Here's how economies in today's marketplaces typically work:

Growth Season (Expansion)

Jobs are plentiful. Businesses are hiring. People feel confident about spending money. Your investments tend to grow. This is when things feel easy.

Peak

This is as good as it gets in the current cycle. Everything feels great. But smart people know that what goes up eventually comes down. Not because they're pessimistic—because they're realistic.

Slowdown (Contraction)

The economy starts cooling off. Companies slow down hiring or start laying people off. People spend less. Investments might lose value. This is a storm season.

Bottom (Trough)

This is the low point. Things feel hard. But here's the good news: This is also where the next growth season begins. Seeds planted here grow strong roots.

Why does this matter to you? Because if you understand these seasons, you won't panic when things get tough. You'll know it's temporary. And you'll be ready.

Your Emergency Savings Fund: Your Financial Shock Absorber

This is the single most important thing you can build to protect yourself from money problems.

An emergency fund is simple: It's money you don't touch unless there's a real emergency. Not a sale. Not a vacation. An actual emergency.

How much do you need?

Start with $1,000. Seriously. Just $1,000 will handle most small emergencies—a car repair, a broken phone, an unexpected bill.

Then work toward three to six months of basic living expenses. That's your rent, groceries, utilities, transportation—the must-haves.

How do you build it? Start small. Even $25 a week adds up to $1,300 in a year. $50 a week? That's $2,600.

Set up automatic transfers from checking to savings. Treat it like a bill you pay to your future self.

Every tax refund, birthday gift, or bonus? Put at least half in your emergency fund. Here's a Grace Challenge. That $25 has all kinds of things asking for attention. But if you act in integrity, then you will be able to withstand saying 'no' to less important expenditures and begin to hold the line on your self-discipline.

Where should you keep it? In a separate savings account. Not your checking account, where you'll accidentally spend it. But also, not locked up in investments you don't want to interrupt or can't easily access.

You want it boring and available. This isn't about growing wealth. It's about having it when you need it and living with the hope of tomorrow tangibly in your patterns.

Smart Debt Habits (Before Debt Becomes a Problem)

The best way to deal with debt? Don't let it pile up in the first place. God's Word is clear! Don't allow yourself to become enslaved by debt, except for the debt to love one another.

The Good, the Bad, and the Ugly

Not all debt is equal. Some debt helps you build something. Some debt just drains you.

Good (Helpful) debt: Helps you build value over time

- A reasonable mortgage (you're building equity)
- Student loans for education that leads to a better income

- A modest car loan for reliable transportation to work

Bad (Harmful) debt: Costs you money but doesn't build value

- High-interest credit cards for stuff you don't need
- Payday loans (these are terrible—avoid them)
- Financing things that lose value immediately (furniture, electronics, etc.)

The Rules to Live By

1. If you can't afford it twice, you can't afford it once. Before buying something on credit, ask: Could I pay for this in cash right now and still be, okay? If not, you probably shouldn't buy it. Seriously consider how you will live without it for a season.

2. Pay off credit cards every month. If you can't, don't use them. The interest will destroy you.

3. Never borrow for wants, only for needs. There's a difference between "I need new shoes because mine have holes" and "I want those $200 sneakers."

4. Have a payoff plan for every debt. Before taking on any debt, know exactly how you'll pay it back.

Debt obligates the future. Those who fail to understand this get themselves into binds that seem to literally bury them. Don't forget, Grace's intent and desire for you is to be free to serve

Multiple Streams: Don't Put All Your Eggs in One Basket

Here's something that took me years to learn: Relying on just one source of income is risky. What happens if you lose your job? What if your hours get cut? What if your industry changes? What if you have to do something to earn money that isn't ideal?

Think about diversifying

Your income:

- Fulltime job
- Part-time side work
- Freelance projects
- Small business

You don't need all of these at once. But having at least one backup option means you're never completely vulnerable.

Your investments (when you get there):

Don't put everything in one place. Spread it around—stocks, bonds, real estate, savings. This isn't about getting rich quickly. It's about not losing everything at once.

Your skills:

Keep learning. The more you can do, the more valuable you are. The job market changes fast. People who keep developing new skills stay employable.

My way of embracing this was to complete the Certified Financial Planner professional education program. It gave me the context to understand what I didn’t know about money and how it works, and how you work it.

Staying Flexible and Informed

The world changes fast. Industries disappear. New opportunities emerge. The people who thrive are the ones who stay flexible. This will be especially true as we head into the quantum world.

Keep learning

Take traditional and online courses, whether for credit or for personal/professional learning. Read books. Watch videos. Attend workshops. Learn new skills. Your education didn't end when school did. If you didn’t like school, get over it, you are on your own now, and learning is a true virtue. Grace will ground your learning with humility and gratitude

Build your network.

Stay connected with people in your field and outside it. Join groups. Go to events. Help people. When opportunity or trouble comes, your network becomes your safety net.

Stay informed (but don't obsess).

Pay attention to what's happening in the economy. Read reliable news sources. But don't let financial news make you anxious. You're looking for trends, not daily panic.

Be willing to pivot.

If the industry you are involved with is struggling, consider related fields. If your skills aren't in demand, add new ones. Flexibility isn't weakness—it's wisdom.

The Mindset That Holds It All Together

Here's the truth: You can have all the right strategies and still struggle if your mindset is working against you. Here are ways to pivot to take your stewardship role seriously.

Focus on what you can control.

You can't control the economy. You can't control whether your company does layoffs. But you can control how prepared you are. You can control your spending. You can control whether you're learning new skills.

Practice Grace's gratitude.

Even when things are tight, there's always something to be grateful for. Gratitude isn't about pretending everything is perfect. It's about recognizing what's good while you work on what needs to change. It's about being thankful for each breath you take.

Remember: This is temporary.

Whatever season you're in—good or bad—it won't last forever. When times are good, save for when they're not. When times are tough, remember that growth is coming.

Trust in Grace.

Your worth isn't determined by your bank account. Your security doesn't come from having everything figured out. Grace meets you where you are and provides what you need—not always what you want, but what you need.

Embracing a Repentant, and Redeemed Community Mindset

When you apply the Grace Formula, you begin to notice how Grace redeems every aspect of life. Not only does the formula ground your decisions in the power and promise of Grace, but it also frames how you live in faith, project ardent hope for better things to come, and grounds you love in a clear image of agape Love, which can be emulated with the help of the Holy Spirit of Grace.

What it requires is a belief in the sufficiency of Grace to guide our decisions for living as a steward of the One who has given us all good things. As you grow in this gift of Grace, you become more able to be formed by the eternal love of God in our Lord and Savior, Jesus Christ.

Nothing was predictable. But we learned to walk into uncertainty with eyes wide open and hearts anchored in hope.

This formula pulls all things together into a uniform and coherent framework under the blueprint that Grace provides, in the economies of life.

Building Your Safety Net: The Practical Checklist

Here's your roadmap. You don't have to do everything at once. Just keep moving forward.

Foundation (Start Here):

- Return your first-fruits with a regular digital transfer
- Save $1,000 emergency savings fund
- Create a monthly spending plan or budget you can stick to
- Pay off any payday loans or high-interest debt
- Set up automatic savings transfers

Building Up (Next Steps):

- Increase emergency savings fund to 3-6 months' expenses
- Pay off credit card debt
- Start or increase retirement contributions
- Learn one new marketable skill or further develop what Grace has given

Getting Strong (Long-Term):

- Maintain a healthy credit score
- Diversify income streams
- Review and adjust investments
- Keep learning and networking
- Recognize that you are called to manage on behalf of the true Owner.

The Bottom Line

Chapter 16 was about surviving the storm. This chapter is about building a house that can withstand the next one.

You're not trying to become rich (though that's fine if it happens). You're trying to build stability. Security. Peace of mind. One faithful and diligent decision after the next.

That comes from:

- Having money set aside for emergencies
- Managing debt wisely
- Diversifying your income and skills

- Staying flexible and informed
- Maintaining the right mindset

Do these things, and you won't just survive economic uncertainties. You'll navigate them with greater confidence. However, let Grace be your sufficiency in all matters of life. Remind yourself that your life was ransomed with a price, and you are treasured by Grace.

Remember: Financial jubilee isn't about having it all figured out. It's about knowing you can handle whatever comes and that Grace will be your anchor to ground you during the storms and sunny days of life.

And with Grace as your grounding, you can.

Key Takeaways

Understand economic seasons. The economy has ups and downs. Neither lasts forever. Knowing this helps you prepare with patterns instead of panic.

Build your emergency savings fund. Start by setting up the mechanics and build to $1,000, then work toward 3-6 months of expenses. This is your financial shock absorber.

Manage debt before it manages you. Not all debt is equal. Avoid bad or harmful debt, minimize good or helpful debt, and always have a payoff plan.

Diversify everything. Your time, identity, income, investments, and skills. Don't put all your eggs in one basket.

Stay flexible and keep learning. The world changes fast. People who adapt persevere and flourish.

For Reflection

What would three to six months of expenses look like for you? Write down the number. Now break it down: How much would you need to save each month to reach that goal in one year?

What's one skill you could develop that would make you more financially secure? What's stopping you from starting to learn it this week?

What help do you need? Who would be an encouraging voice for you? How does the Grace Formula help?

"Uncertainty doesn't always mean instability. Learn how to flourish in difficult times. The Grace Formula and the Grace-Flow movement hope to encourage and equip."

Chapter 18

Provision in Every Season

When I was a young boy trying to become a man, I learned how to keep money flowing to meet my and my family's needs. My father showed me how to live within my means and save, while raising 11 children—first in India, then in America after we moved when I was 12.

Dad taught me to budget and track every dollar. That was a huge gift. But what I didn't learn was how money actually works and how to make it work for you. There never seemed to be enough margin. Looking back, I can see what I missed: I didn't build in a real savings plan.

I paid attention when financial experts talked, though. I established a relationship with an insurance advisor and started saving with mutual funds while I saved emergency reserves. When I got married, hoping for children, I bought a life insurance policy—really a love letter in Grace, to my wife, and our future children.

My own investing took a sharp turn when I jumped back into the Social Security system (see Chapter 16). Life was messy. Cash flow was always tight. Sacrifices would have to be made.

But Grace—God's Grace—kept shining light in my and Melede's hearts, motivating us to live according to the Grace Formula. I didn't get there overnight, but with consistent decisions, we journeyed with bumps that were smoothed with joy and peace.

The key was that in faith through Grace, we recognized that Grace was sufficient for the day, and *God's Grace is made perfect in our weakness.* (2 Corinthians 12:9 ESV). Grace is true balm for the cutting sting of guilt and a sense of guilt.

We began living seasonally. Our finances followed suit—paced with purpose.

The Changing Priorities of Life

You've learned the fundamentals—financial discipline when money's tight (Chapter 16), Grace Gives You Enough as you build your safety net (Chapter 17). Those essential steps are super important to respect and form. If they are equivalent to the Grace that gives all good things, then Grace grounds most other decisions.

The fundamentals or key patterns don't change much. What *does* change? Your priorities. Your questions. Where you direct your attention and resources. Your energy levels and your advocate are always restocked.

A 25-year-old asking, "Should I rent or buy?" faces completely different decisions than a 45-year-old asking, "How do I help my kids pay for college?" And both differ from a 65-year-old wondering, "Can I actually retire?" Same foundational basics. Different life stages. Different questions, yet important choices.

This chapter walks through the major financial transitions most people face—helping you see what matters most at each turn in the road.

Starting (Ages 18-30): Setting Your Direction

This season is about establishing patterns that will serve you for decades.

The Big Question: "What kind of life am I building?"

You're probably either in college or early in your working years and career. Your income is likely the lowest it will ever be—but so are your responsibilities. This is your window.

What Matters Most Right Now

Invest in your earning power. Your biggest asset isn't your savings—it's your ability to earn income for the next 40 years. Should you take that certification course? Learn new software?

Consider moving to a population area with better opportunities? These decisions compound. A $5,000 investment in skills that increase your income by $10,000 per year pays for itself in six months—and keeps paying for decades.

Start charitable contributions early—even small ones. Expressing your faith may feel less important at 25, but here's the benefit: $100 per month given from age 25 to 35 (just 10 years, $12,000 total) and cast upon the fields ripe for harvest, will be used by the Holy Spirit of Grace to increase the Kingdom of Grace's growth to more than $400 per month invested from age 35 to 65 (30 years, $144,000 total). Even though the Creator of the Universe doesn't need our money, when cast against the background of our life's purpose, it will redound to the benefit of our own lives to live out our faith to project its priority. Start now, even small.

Start retirement contributions early—start the pattern now to benefit from the compounding of time. Retirement feels distant at 25, but here's the math: $200 per month invested from age 25 to 35 (just 10 years, $24,000 total) and left alone will likely grow to more than $200 per month invested from age 35 to 65 (30 years, $72,000 total). Start now, even small.

Date members of the opposite gender before you marry. Experience treating your date in a way that reflects Grace. If the other person is a Grace-grounded person, they will be more attracted to your values lived with integrity. Don't see this as a time to get what you can, but rather as a time to practice the patterns that don't keep God's Grace to yourself but let your light shine. In this way, you will put your trust not in the temporal things that change and vacillate with personal urges or desires. If you want a spouse who is a Grace-filled person, then this integrity will protect you before big commitments like taking responsibility for another, a mortgage, or an expensive lifestyle. Flexibility in integrity is Grace's power right now. Use it.

The Trap to Avoid

Lifestyle inflation. You get your first real paycheck and suddenly "need" a nicer apartment, a new car, and dinners out constantly. Before you know it, you're making twice as much but have less margin than before. The pattern you establish now becomes increasingly harder to change.

Building a Family (Ages 30-45): Managing Competing Commitments

This can be the squeeze season. Career advancement, homeownership, raising kids, aging parents, retirement savings—all at once.

The Big Question: "How do I balance everyone's needs, including my own?"

Everything costs more than expected. Childcare. Healthcare. Housing. Education. And somehow, you're supposed to save for retirement while your kid needs braces and your roof needs replacing.

What Matters Most Right Now

Protect the people Grace has provided. Unselfishness becomes a key here. Prioritizing the needs of others becomes a key motivator. Life insurance becomes critical when others depend on your income. Term life insurance is affordable and straightforward enough to replace your income for 10-20 years. Don't overthink it. Get it. Disability insurance matters too—you're more likely to become disabled than die young.

Housing decisions have long shadows. Buy when you plan to stay 5-7 years, have an emergency fund beyond your down payment, and total housing costs are manageable. The wrong house at the wrong time can trap you financially for years. Remember that this is a shelter, not a showcase.

Education planning requires early decisions. If college matters, start a 529 plan early. Even $100 monthly adds up over 18 years. But here's the hard truth: your retirement comes before their college. They can borrow for education. You can't borrow for retirement.

Career advancement matters now. This is your peak earning season. The moves you make between 35 and 50—job changes, promotions, and skill development—create most of your lifetime wealth. Stay marketable. Take calculated risks.

The Trap to Avoid

Trying to do everything perfectly at once. You can't max retirement accounts, fully fund 529s, pay off your mortgage early, and maintain an ideal emergency fund simultaneously. Prioritize: 1) Basic emergency fund and insurance, 2) Employer retirement match, 3) Other goals by importance. Adjust as life changes.

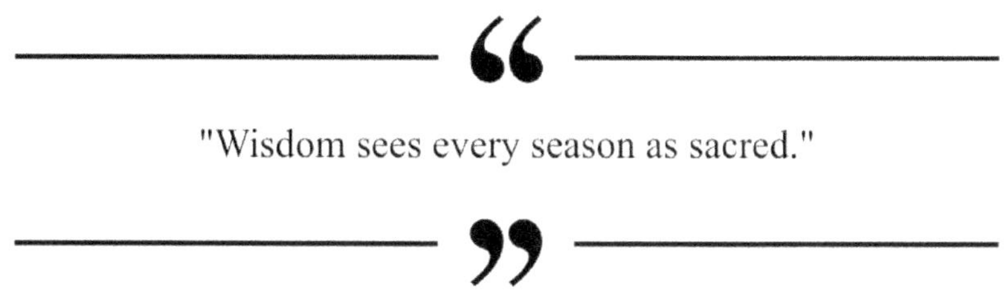

"Wisdom sees every season as sacred."

Approaching Retirement (Ages 50-65): Shifting Gears

Your kids are likely grown. Your income is probably at its peak. Retirement is within sight.

The Big Question: "Am I actually ready for this?"

Many people panic here, realizing they're 15 years from retirement without adequate savings, or they've saved but don't know if it's sufficient. The other side of this coin is that we have more than sufficient resources, but fail to love our neighbors as ourselves and so we pull our concerns inward rather than seeing our resources as an opportunity to serve others and build the Kingdom of Grace.

What Matters Most Right Now

Run the numbers honestly. How much have you saved? How much do you need? Rough rule: You'll need about 25 times your annual expenses saved to retire comfortably using the 4% withdrawal rule. If you need $50,000 yearly beyond Social Security, you'll need roughly $1.25 million saved. Know where you stand, but also know what you can do today to move in that direction.

Catch-up contributions are your friend. At 50, you can contribute extra to retirement accounts. If you're behind, maximize these.

Think through healthcare. You can't get Medicare until 65. If you retire before that, how will you cover insurance? COBRA and private insurance are expensive. Health Savings Accounts are powerful if eligible. Look at the collectives that are developing cost-effective alternatives. Healthcare costs can derail retirement plans.

Shift your risk gradually. If most retirement savings remain in aggressive investments, slowly shift some to conservative options. You don't want a major market downturn right before retirement. But don't abandon growth—you might live 30+ more years. Here is where the counsel of many advisors can be useful.

Define what retirement means. Retirement isn't just financial—it's an identity shift. For 40+ years, work structured your days and provided purpose. What replaces that? Many of the happiest and most fulfilled people retire *to* something, not just *from* something. This is indeed a vocation with great opportunities to make life better for those around you.

The Trap to Avoid

Assuming you'll "figure it out" in retirement. Decisions about Social Security claiming, account withdrawals, and healthcare have permanent consequences. Changes to these landscapes are in turbulent years. Unfortunately, we have sacrificed over 70 million of our own children to the altar of personal choice. Remember that Grace offers forgiveness and a Jubilee to come. Seek out spiritual and professional help as needed.

In Retirement (Ages 65+): Managing What Grace has Provided

You've spent 40+ years building on the patterns that reflect your priorities and values. Now you're managing and distributing.

The Big Question: "Will the funds available to you last as long as you do?"

This is the season of withdrawal strategies, required minimum distributions, Medicare decisions, and estate plans.

What Matters Most Right Now

Create a sustainable withdrawal plan. If you have a pension, you have this benefit often at the expense of being able to allocate and save directly in the marketplace. The 4% rule is a sound conservative starting point: withdraw 4% of your retirement savings portfolio in year one, then adjust for inflation yearly. Work with an advisor to account for your specific tax situation and spending needs.

Understand Social Security options. When you claim dramatically affects what you receive. Claim at 62 for reduced benefits for life. Wait until 70 for maximum benefits. For many, waiting is worth it—especially if healthy. If married, coordinate with your spouse's strategy.

As we look to the future of the government social security system, there is much to be concerned about. What will I do if that system isn't sustainable? How will I pivot when Social Security doesn't provide as much, or not at all?

This decision, like all others, should be grounded in the Grace that sustains and provides sufficiency today and tomorrow. Don't let this assurance keep you from planning as a steward of assets given to you by Grace.

Don't forget taxes. Traditional IRAs, 401(k)s, or 403bs are taxed as ordinary income when withdrawn. Roth IRAs are tax-free but require post-tax assets. Social Security might be taxable depending on other income. Consider tax implications for each dollar withdrawn. If you have a tax advisor, lean on their guidance.

Plan for long-term care. Most people need some form of long-term care eventually—home health aides, assisted living, or nursing homes. It's expensive, and Medicare doesn't cover most. Long-term care insurance is one option. Some self-fund. Have a plan.

Think about Heritage. What do you want to leave behind? For many, this isn't just money—it's values, faith, and impact. Get estate planning, wills, trusts, and beneficiary designations in order. They're gifts to loved ones.

If your faith community has charitable planning counselors, take advantage of their help. Most people make these plans without ever considering the full scope of opportunity. If your attorney doesn't ask about your faith, hope, and love, witness to the Grace that you have received.

The Trap to Avoid

One common snare that often inhibits is spending too conservatively out of fear. Yes, make your money last. But live in a way that is equivalent to Grace during your working years as in your retirement. If you've saved for decades—find balance between security and fulfillment.

The Thread That Runs Through Every Stage

At every age, the Grace Formula applies:

Faith (___%)

Trust that it is God's Grace who provides for and guides your decisions.

Hope (___%)

Project forward with confidence that tomorrow can be better. Action this hope.

Love (___%)

Ground every financial decision in the Love that comes from Grace—for God, for others, for the life you're called to live.

Grace (100%)

Recognize that your sufficiency comes not from perfect planning but from the One who provides all that we need for this life and holds all things together.

Financial decision-making across life stages isn't about perfect answers at 25 that carry you to 85. It's about paying attention to what matters most *right now*, while keeping an eye on what's coming next.

Key Takeaways

Different stages, different priorities. The mechanics stay the same, but your focus shifts dramatically from your twenties to retirement.

Timing matters. Some decisions—like starting retirement savings or buying life insurance—are far more powerful when made early. Others—like Social Security claiming—require patience and strategy.

Protect what matters. Insurance protects the people and things you love with discounted costs but leveraged returns. It's an act of love, not fear.

Invest in your earning power. Especially early on, money spent on skills and opportunities compounds for decades.

Get help when needed. Some decisions have permanent consequences. Seek qualified and spiritual guidance. Remember that we are not just flesh and blood; we all have a spirit. If your spirit is light, then recognize such Grace. If your spirit is dark, seek the help of others whom you trust. Either way, Grace waits at the door.

For Reflection

What life stage are you in right now?

What's the one financial priority you should be focusing on that you've been avoiding? What challenges keep getting stuck?

How does the Grace Formula help you approach financial decision-making with contentment, then diligence, instead of anxiety?

Chapter 19

Calm When Money Feels Overwhelming

Money became important to me, but when I turned 50, the stakes felt even higher. Did I have catching up to do? Absolutely. Did I stress out about it? More than I'd like to admit.

Here's the thing about being in the thick of it—you can't see the forest for the trees. I had been preparing for the future, adjusting my patterns, but something didn't feel right. I had no real context for my decisions, so I decided to learn.

That led me to complete the professional education program used to train Certified Financial Planners. Six rigorous courses. They helped with my charitable planning work, but I had no idea what this knowledge would do for my confidence. Suddenly, I could assess various issues and see how different pieces fit together—how one decision affects another, how timing matters, how risk and reward balance out.

This confidence builder supercharged my journey and made a tremendous difference.

But it wasn't until I went back into God's revealed Word that I found the wisdom I'd been searching for. Suddenly it all came together. Embedded in God's Word are all the kernels of wisdom and know-how I needed to be faithful.

As someone who had learned about my character defects, I asked Grace to forgive me, guide me, and give me comfort as I continued to make hard choices to protect me and those I loved dearly.

Looking back on this time in my journey, I began to recognize a fuller scope of God's Economies.

Within the economies of Grace, there are no transactions we bring to the table—only the one transaction God made for all humans when Jesus, the Christ, Grace in Flesh, gave up His life for mine and yours. That realization firmly entrenched within me a clearer sense of my identity as a baptized child of Grace.

Since that time, I've been carried along with the winds of eternal joy and peace. The Jubilee that Grace has in mind for us is here today, and it will be here tomorrow and forever. How priceless is that! You will find Grace in audible and tangible means at the Altar. Wise men and women still seek Him.

Change became not just something to survive—but a call to adjust.

Change no longer felt like loss alone—it became a call to adjust, to grow into someone who could carry love more boldly.

Standing at the Crossroads

Maybe you're in your late thirties now, juggling a career, family responsibilities, maybe some aging parents, perhaps kids heading toward college or pets. Life feels like a whirlwind of possibilities and pressures.

You stand at a unique crossroads in your economic journey—a place where embracing change can lead not just to economic stability but also to personal confidence. You might feel a mix of excitement and anxiety about this transition. That's perfectly normal. Change can be intimidating, but it can also spark incredible opportunity and growth.

Just remember opportunity and growth come with risk.

But here's what's often missing from that equation: trust. Not just trust in your own abilities or in market trends, but trust in Grace—the kind of trust that allows you to release control without becoming careless, to face your financial reality honestly without shame, and to move forward with peace instead of panic.

Why Silent Anxiety Erodes Trust

Money creates a quiet distance between us and God, and between us and each other. You might not talk about your financial fears with your spouse. You probably don't bring them honestly to God in prayer. And you certainly don't share them at church or with friends.

This silence isn't neutral. Trust erodes in it.

Many of your financial fears weren't even yours to begin with—they were inherited. Maybe you grew up hearing "money doesn't grow on trees" or watching parents argue about bills. These scarcity narratives shaped your financial sensitivities, while faith competed for space.

The problem is, when we moralize money and turn struggle into spiritual failure, shame replaces stewardship. And shame doesn't produce change—Grace does.

God Is Not Afraid of Your Numbers

Here's a truth that might surprise you: **Trust begins with honesty, not improvement.**

God is not afraid of your numbers. Not your debt. Not your income. Not your mistakes. Not your confusion about whether you're doing this right.

You don't need to edit your financial reality or perform spiritual confidence you don't feel. You can invite God fully into your economic situation exactly as it is right now.

This is where real change begins—not in having it all figured out, but in trusting that Grace meets you in the mess.

Taking Stock: Your Economies Health Check-Up

Just as you get a physical health check-up, you need an economies health check-up. But let's approach this differently than typical financial advice. This isn't about shame or comparison.

This is about humble and honest assessment that builds trust.

Calculate your financial net worth. List all your assets—your home, savings, investments—and subtract your liabilities like debts and mortgages. As you do this, notice your emotional response. Is there shame? Fear? Resistance? Bring those feelings to God honestly. Remember: trust begins with honesty, not improvement.

Review your income sources. List everything—your salary, any side income, rental income, dividends, passive income streams. Then ask yourself: Will these income sources support the lifestyle I want in the coming years? Don't let this question spiral into anxiety. Instead, let it be an honest conversation with God about provision.

Analyze your spending. Dive deep into your monthly expenses. Where could you cut back? This isn't about judgment. Many of us were never taught how to manage money well. This is your chance to identify patterns without shame and create space for rational thought instead of emotional reactions.

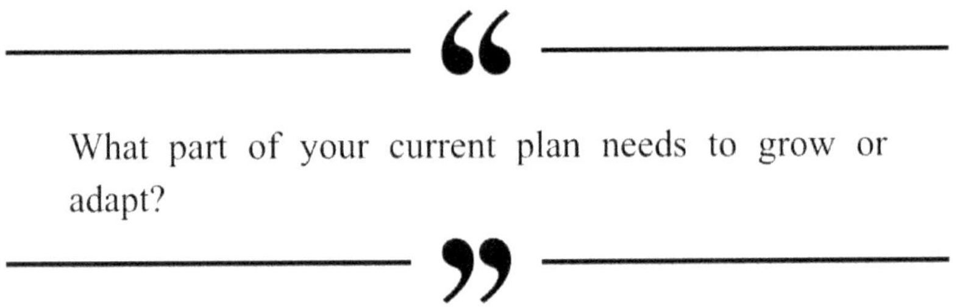

From Scarcity to Sufficiency

The shift from scarcity thinking to sufficiency thinking was covered fully in Chapter 7. Here, the practical application is this: when you approach your economies health check-up from a posture of scarcity, every number feels like a verdict. When you approach it from sufficiency—trusting that Grace provides what you need—the same numbers become information rather than condemnation. That posture changes what you're able to do with what you find.

Sufficiency is spiritual maturity, not financial excess.

You don't need to be wealthy to experience God's provision. You need to shift from a scarcity mindset—"there's never enough"—to a sufficiency mindset: "God provides what I need."

This doesn't mean ignoring real financial challenges. It means anchoring your peace in Grace rather than in your bank account balance.

When you operate from scarcity, every financial decision feels desperate. But when you operate from sufficiency—trusting that God sees your needs and provides—you can make clearer, calmer decisions.

Grace Before Discipline

We covered this in Chapter 6, and it bears noting again here without repeating it at length: structure and discipline only hold when Grace comes first. If you find yourself white-knuckling a budget or gritting through a savings plan, the problem is rarely the plan. Go back to the foundation. Let Grace precede the discipline, not the other way around.

Adjust your budget. If your current budgeting method isn't working, revamp it. It's absolutely crucial to track your ins and outs rather than relying on feelings or random thoughts to guide you.

But do this from a place of trust, not control. You're not trying to squeeze every penny out of guilt. You're stewarding what God has entrusted to you with penitential wisdom and care.

Tackle your debt. If debts are hanging over your head, create a strategy to address them. Debt can be a form of bondage. Consider consolidating high-interest debts or prioritizing payments on those that weigh heaviest. The goal is to lighten your load—not through frantic effort that leaves you exhausted, but through steady, Grace-grounded action. Seek support from reputable professional advisors and organizations within the business community to help develop a debt management plan that allows you to move forward. This is an area that can lead to many unnecessary costs.

Evaluate your investments. Are your investments aligned with your current risk tolerance and economic goals? Remember: trust grows through practice, not pressure. You don't have to get this perfect. You just need to take the next faithful step.

Building Trust Through Practice

Saying "I trust God" is different from learning to walk in trust daily. **Trust is built, not declared.**

Trust grows through small, repeated practices—not dramatic leaps of faith. Change happens in unseen inches, not visible leaps.

Talk about money without losing relationships. One of the most important practices is learning how to create safe conversations about money with God, your spouse, children, faith leaders, and community. Trust deepens through humble dialogue. Don't let silence erode your most important relationships.

Connect with others. Engage with peers and mentors who share your love, interests and faith. Collaborating with others can open doors to fresh perspectives and new opportunities.

Keep learning. Economic literacy is a journey without a finish line. Seek out resources that can deepen your understanding. Knowledge is useful, but wisdom—the ability to see the context in Grace clearly and with purpose—is better. Take a close look at your understanding of the 100% of Grace. Reflect on how that core truth motivates your decision-making.

Contentment as a Spiritual Posture

One of the most powerful shifts you can make is learning to rest from financial anxiety. **Contentment is a spiritual posture before it's a financial outcome.**

You can practice releasing control without becoming careless. This is the art of faithful stewardship—doing what you can while trusting God with what you cannot control.

Write down your economic fears. Acknowledging them can

diminish their power. Don't hesitate to reach out to family, friends, or professional confidants for guidance. Engage in spiritual practices that center you—prayers, Scripture reading, meditation, deep breathing. These aren't just stress-management techniques. They're ways of repositioning your heart to trust God's provision and timing in Grace. Grace meets us in the wilderness. May we find sufficiency there, in our weakness.

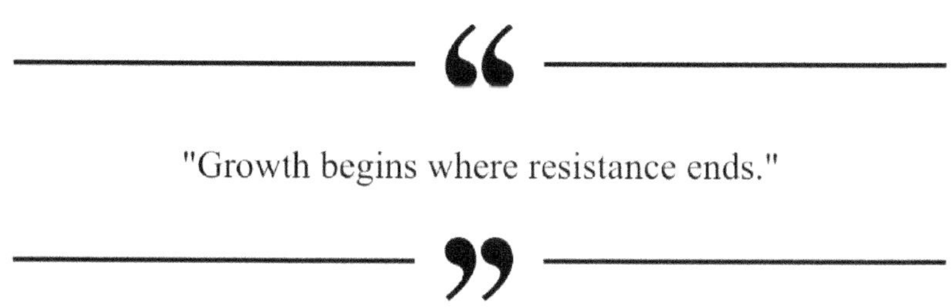

"Growth begins where resistance ends."

Small Acts That Rebuild Confidence

As you navigate financial changes, faithful trust is revealed in simple, repeated practices. You don't need dramatic breakthroughs. You need consistent, small steps.

Define your goals. Establish specific, measurable, achievable, relevant, and time-bound (SMART) economic goals. Create an action plan with actionable steps and deadlines. If you have a hard time getting to these planning details, ask a coach or trusted partner to help you.

Reflect regularly. Schedule regular check-ins with yourself to assess progress. Reflecting on your journey with gratitude will help you stay aligned and adjust, as necessary.

This isn't about perfect execution. It's about faithful presence—showing up to steward what God has given you, one day at a time.

Calm Stewardship in Changing Markets and Seasons

Stay informed about market movements but remember: **Calm stewardship speaks louder than success stories.** Your financial peace—even in uncertainty—quietly testifies to faith in a striving world. People notice when you're not frantic, not desperate, not driven by fear.

Diversify your investments across various sectors and asset classes. Review and rebalance periodically to ensure alignment with your values, goals, risk tolerance, and time horizons.

Moving Forward

Celebrate your wins. Maintain a journal to document your economic accomplishments, both big and small. This serves as motivation during challenging times and a reminder to practice gratitude when times provide surplus.

Learn from mistakes with Grace. Analyze past economic decisions that didn't pan out. Reflect on what went wrong and how you can avoid similar pitfalls. Be kind to yourself. Everyone makes economic missteps. It may also signal a need to have more accountability. If you are afraid of this, be careful, be humble. Remember: shame doesn't produce change—Grace does.

Keep adjusting. Periodically reassess your economic goals. Remain flexible. Be open to changing course if new opportunities or challenges arise.

Trust as Journey, Not Destination

Healed trust in Grace becomes the doorway to generosity, unity, and heritage. **Trust is not the destination—it's the journey.**

As you stand at this crossroads in your journey through the economies of life, remember that embracing change and growth isn't ultimately about achieving financial success. It's about learning to rest in God's provision, walk with justice and humility in kind stewardship, and experience the contented peace that comes from trusting Grace.

Your economic journey is uniquely yours, filled with opportunities for learning, growth, downfalls and deepening trust. Embrace this journey as you nurture a future aligned with your deepest values and

God's calling on your life.

Your economic future is bright—not because you'll get everything right, but because Grace is already 100%.

Question for Reflection:

What is one area of financial anxiety you're ready to bring honestly to God today, trusting that Grace meets you exactly where you are?

Chapter 20

Living Intentionally

Life in your twenties feels like spinning plates. You're managing work, relationships, dreams for the future—and somehow keeping your finances from falling apart. Some days you wonder if you're doing any of it right.

As a young teacher, I juggled countless priorities—lesson plans, grading, staff meetings, athletic administration. Then I married Melede, and everything shifted. My time wasn't just mine anymore. I had sacred responsibilities: to my students, to my calling, and to my sacred partnership with her.

Those early years taught me something crucial: living intentionally isn't about controlling everything. It's about recognizing Grace in the chaos and making choices that honor what truly matters. Financial decisions? They're no different.

Every decision became a meditation. Grace slowed my soul.

Here's what we're going to explore together: how living intentionally with your money can change everything. Not just your bank account, but your whole relationship with finances and the concord and peace you feel about your future.

When Money Meets Intention

Being intentional means living fully present in this moment. You notice your thoughts and feelings without beating yourself up about them. You acknowledge what's happening in your mind and heart while staying grounded in right now.

This isn't just about meditation or breathing exercises. It's a whole different way of making financial decisions—one rooted in Grace-awareness. When you're aware of God's Grace-Flowing through your life, you approach money differently.

Today's world moves fast. Bills stack up. Savings goals feel impossible. You're always waiting for the other shoe to drop—another unexpected expense around the corner. Living with Grace-awareness helps you slow down and approach your finances with purpose and clarity.

When you bring intention to your money decisions, you stop reacting out of fear or panic. Instead, you make choices that line up with what actually matters to you and where you want to go long-term.

Why Grace Awareness Changes Financial Decisions

Living intentionally with money—staying Grace-aware—opens your eyes to why you do what you do with your finances. This requires you to learn the power and promise of divine Grace. God wants you to experience His Jubilee. Search the Scriptures for they testify about the Grace and Truth that is in Jesus Christ. Here's what makes it essential:

You understand your emotions. Money triggers feelings—fear, guilt, pride, sometimes even joy. When you're Grace-aware, you recognize these emotions. You understand why you might overspend or why you hesitate to invest. Instead of letting feelings drive your decisions, you respond thoughtfully.

You focus better. Practicing intentionality trains your brain to concentrate on what's in front of you. This sharper focus helps you sort through financial information and prioritize what really matters. You're less likely to get distracted by quick wins that sabotage your long-term goals.

You reduce stress. Money anxiety is real. But Grace-awareness helps calm that anxiety. You learn to respond to stress with a clear head instead of panic. This emotional strength helps you make decisions from a stable place, not from fear.

"Grace awareness turns transactions into sacred moments."

”

Getting Started: Intentional Spending

The first step is becoming aware of your spending habits and lining them up with your values.

Here's how:

Track every dollar for a month. Write it all down either on paper on in a spreadsheet or an automated tracking program. This shows you patterns you didn't know existed. You'll spot areas where money disappears on things that don't actually matter to you.

Figure out your values. Spend some time thinking about what truly matters to you. What do you care about? What do you want to prioritize in your life? Once you're clear on your values, you can make spending choices that reflect them.

Pause before you buy. Before making a purchase, stop for a moment and practice Grace-awareness. Ask yourself:

- Does this fit with my priority beliefs and values?
- How will I feel about this purchase next week? Next month?
- Am I buying this out of habit or impulse, or do I genuinely need it?

Making Saving Feel Different

Saving money doesn't have to feel like punishment. When you approach it intentionally, saving becomes something positive, rather than drudgery.

Get specific about goals. Don't just save for "someday." Are you saving for a trip? A car? An emergency savings fund? Set concrete targets and deadlines. This keeps your motivation alive.

Automate it. Set up automatic transfers to your savings account. When saving happens automatically, you don't have to think about it. It stops feeling like a burden.

See your dreams. Create a vision board or digital collection of your savings goals. Seeing what you're working toward is powerful motivation. It reminds you why this matters.

Intentional Investing

Investing intimidates a lot of people, especially when you're new to personal finance. But bringing Grace awareness to your investment strategy helps you make smarter decisions:

Learn the basics. Take time to understand different investment options. Know the risks and potential returns of stocks, bonds, mutual funds, and other choices. Knowledge gives you power to choose well.

Think about what you want your investments to accomplish. Retirement? A house? Starting a business someday? Line up your investments with your life goals.

Stay patient. Markets go up and down. That's normal. An intentional investor recognizes that fluctuations are part of the deal. Instead of panicking when the market dips, focus on your long-term strategy and stick with it.

Handling Financial Stress with Grace-awareness

Money anxiety shows up for most people, especially in uncertain times. Acknowledging and addressing this anxiety matters for your mental health. Here are strategies that help:

Breathe deeply-Pause-Pray. When financial worry creeps in, pause, pray and practice deep breathing. Inhale slowly through your nose, hold for a few seconds, exhale slowly through your mouth. This simple practice calms your mind and reduces stress. While you are at this, pray that you will breathe in the Holy Spirit of Grace to calm your troubled spirit.

Create a clear action plan. Write out a plan for managing your finances. Include your budget, savings goals, and debt payoff strategies. Having structure helps ease anxiety because you feel more in control. Set yourself up for Grace. Small steps, consistently, contentedly, confessionally.

Limit financial news. Staying informed matters, but constant exposure to negative financial news increases anxiety. Set boundaries around how much financial news you consume. This protects your mindset and preserves your Grace-awareness. Consider replacing that with God's Word.

Talking About Money Intentionally

Money conversations feel uncomfortable, especially with family and friends. But open, honest communication is vital for healthy financial relationships. Here's how to approach these talks with Grace-awareness:

Pick the right moment. Find a comfortable environment to discuss finances. Avoid stressful settings. Make sure everyone has time for a real conversation.

Really listen. During money discussions, focus on truly hearing the other person's perspective. Show empathy and understanding. This leads to better conversations.

Be transparent. Share your thoughts and feelings about money openly. Honesty builds trust and strengthens relationships. It lets you work through financial matters together.

Building Daily Practices

Weaving intention and Grace-awareness into your daily routine reinforces a positive mindset toward finances. Try these practices:

Morning reflection. Start your day with a few quiet minutes. Set intentions for your financial choices throughout the day. Remind yourself of your values and goals. Acknowledge the Grace that surrounds you.

Gratitude journaling. Keep a journal where you list things you appreciate, including financial aspects of your life. Recognizing what you have shifts your focus from scarcity to sufficiency—from fear to Grace-awareness.

Evening review. At day's end, review your financial decisions intentionally. What went well? What could improve? This helps you learn from each day and keep growing.

Abe's Evening Inquiries-Nightly review changed how he returned, spent, and felt.

Abe, a 38-year-old manager, started asking himself three questions each night: "Where did Grace show up today? What did I spend? What could I return tomorrow?" Within weeks, his impulse purchases dropped, his charitable returning doubled, and his financial anxiety melted away.

Using Tools Intentionally

Technology can support your journey toward greater financial intentionality as a steward. Apps exist for budgeting, tracking expenses, and setting savings goals. Find tools that work for you and simplify your financial management.

Moving Forward with Grace

Living intentionally with your finances—maintaining Grace-awareness in your money decisions—can transform your emotional and mental well-being. When you recognize how Grace, intention, and finances connect, you develop a complete approach to stewardship that lines up with your values and dreams.

As you move through your financial journey, remember it's about progress, not perfection. You'll face challenges. But when you approach them with intention and Grace-awareness, you build resilience and confidence.

Key Take Away

Intentional spending: Track your expenses and line up purchases with your values. Pause before buying to make sure it reflects your true needs and desires. Practice Grace-awareness in your daily financial choices.

Managing stress: Practice deep breathing, create a financial action plan, and limit negative financial news to handle money stress effectively. Let Grace-awareness calm your anxiety.

Open conversations: Have honest discussions about money with family and friends. Choose the right environment, listen carefully, and be transparent to strengthen financial relationships.

Question for Reflection

How can you bring more intention and Grace-awareness into your financial decision-making to create a more purposeful and fulfilling financial journey?

Chapter 21

Grace as Foundation

By now, you've probably experienced your share of ups and downs. Maybe you've watched the economic roller-coaster while trying to figure out your own financial path. Perhaps you've changed careers, started a family, or found yourself wondering if you're making the right choices with your money and time.

When the Equation Finally Made Sense

It kept coming back to me. I had seen the 10 + 10 + 80 pattern many times during my years of helping people organize their charitable planning, and I used these percentages as a guide for my own finances too. Still, something was missing.

Without the summ (100%), the formula isn't a formula at all.

The Grace Formula is true and clear: **100 = 10 + 10 + 80.** In the same way, the Grace Formula is: **Grace = Faith + Hope + Love. These interactive** true equations are fitting to visualize that God's Grace is His Holiness. Divine Grace is the 100% Life @Jubilee Junction™.

Math came fairly easily when I was young. As a teacher, I enjoyed helping others understand mathematical concepts and truths. One of the basic rules of math is simple: if an equation doesn't balance, it's not true—it's false. If the formula doesn't work, it's telling you something.

Later, as I worked to shape my own life around this 10-10-80 framework, I realized that for it to be a true equation, 100% would be required. If the first 10% represents our expression of faith (what we return), then the second 10% represents hope (what we save for our future). With those two pieces in place, the only thing left would be love—the 80% that encompasses how we live most of our lives. Hopefully our lives flow with Grace to others as we reflect the perfect Agape Love of God.

But what did it all add up to?

When I thought about the many ways things eventually worked out—how we were able to continue through hardships, how doors opened when we needed them. As I pondered on how provision came from unexpected places—it occurred to me that the 100% on the product side of the equation had to be **Grace**. Grace from the Creator who sustains, redeems, makes right, and makes life full.

That's when everything clicked into place.

100% Grace = 10% Faith + 10% Hope + 80% Love

This wasn't just a math problem. It was a map for living. The economic teaching and wisdom in Scripture offered everything that people would ever need to faithfully steward the life and resources that we are called to manage as the Creator directed. God's Call to 'work' (care and nurture) and 'keep' (protect) so that everything under our stewardship flourishes to be all that it was created to be. Stewardship either includes all of life, or it involves none of it.

Here's what I've learned after 40 years on life's highways, boulevards, paved, gravel or dirt streets: **managing money isn't just about spreadsheets and savings accounts.** It's about how you use your time and whether you're living in a way that reflects the glow and flows of Grace to serve others and honor The Grace of Your Creation, your Baptism, your Calling, and Your Weakness.

Your financial life—actually, your whole economic life—is either deeply connected to what you believe, what you value, and how you relate to the people around you... or it's a disconnected set of default decisions that have just rolled forward into today.

And here's the part that might surprise you: **true financial freedom comes from Grace.**

That's where our equation comes in: **Grace = Faith + Hope + Love.** Managing your resources well requires more than just practical steps and good habits. It requires a shift in how you accept and think—recognizing that your financial well-being is tied to your emotional and spiritual well-being, too.

Let me walk you through what this equation means, not just for your wallet but for your whole life.

Faith, at this stage of the journey, looks different than it did when we first introduced the formula. It has become trust—the kind that's been tested and held.

Hope is no longer abstract; it's the lived experience of continuing to save, plan, and lean forward even when the road looked uncertain.

Love—the 80% is where most of life happens: in the daily decisions about how to use what we have for the people we love and the world we want to leave better than we found it.

These aren't new definitions. They are the same three—the same formula—now worn in by experience. If Chapter 1 introduced the Grace Formula as a blueprint, this chapter is what it looks like after decades of building with it.

Applying Grace to Your Financial Decisions

So, how do you actually live this out? How do you take faith, hope, and love and make real financial choices with them? **Start with awareness.** You're not just managing numbers—you're managing the resources that allow you to live a meaningful life. Every financial decision reflects your spiritual, moral, civil, or ceremonial values.

Faith questions:

- Am I making decisions from trust or from fear?
- Do I believe that taking small steps forward matters?
- Can I let go of guilt about past mistakes and start fresh?

Hope questions:

- What am I still dreaming about for my future?
- Am I planning for a life I truly want to live?
- Where do I need to adjust my expectations to match reality?

Love questions:

- Am I taking care of myself along with caring for others?
- Do my spending choices reflect what I truly believe and value?
- Where do I need better boundaries to protect my whole well-being?

Sarah's Story: Grace in Action

Sarah, a woman in her mid-thirties, lost her job during an economic downturn. Overwhelmed and anxious, she wasn't sure how she'd make it through.

Then she discovered the 100-10-10-80 framework.

Despite having limited resources, Sarah started returning 10% to causes she cared about. This shifted her focus from what she lacked to what she still had. She began saving 10%—even small amounts—by setting up automatic transfers. Watching her savings grow gave her hope.

The remaining 80% covered her living expenses. Instead of trying to maintain her old lifestyle, Sarah embraced simpler living. Rather than focusing on internet shopping, she focused on what truly mattered rather than keeping up appearances.

Sarah also volunteered her time, helping others in similar situations. This expanded her network and lifted her spirits.

Eventually, she found a new job with better stability and fulfillment. Looking back, Sarah realized her struggles had taught her invaluable lessons about money, faith, and Grace.

By trusting the framework—100% Grace = 10% Faith + 10% Hope + 80% Love—Sarah found financial liberty. Not because her circumstances were perfect, but because she learned to manage her resources with purpose and intention that reflected the light of Grace given to her.

Her story shows how Grace can transform your financial life, even in difficult seasons

Grace in Action: Practical Steps

Speaking practically with you. Here's how to weave faith, hope, and love into your actual financial life:

Faith in Action: Review your financial situation to capture the facts of the matter, honestly. Do you have a plan? If not, create a simple one. If you do, does it still fit your life? Faith doesn't mean ignoring reality—it means trusting that you can handle whatever you discover and make needed changes. Think of that contribution that you've been wanting to share. Don't forget that Grace is present with you!

Hope in Action: Set one or two goals that excite you. Not goals you "should" have, but goals you really want. Maybe it's a trip you've always dreamed of taking. It could be getting rid of a particular debt. Making a purchase you've been eyeing. Maybe it's starting a small business. Perhaps it's being able to retire at 65. Whatever it is, let it pull you forward.

Love in Action: Look at where your money is actually going. Does your spending reflect what matters most to you? Cut back on things that don't align with your values so you can invest more in what brings you fullness in life. And be kind to yourself and others in the process.

The Grace You're Missing

Here's what I want you to hear:

Grace isn't something you earn. It's something you receive.

You don't have to get everything right in order to deserve financial jubilee. You don't have to work yourself to the ground before you're allowed to rest. You don't have to sacrifice everything for everyone else before you matter.

In Grace—You are already valuable. You are already loved. You are already enough.

When you start making financial decisions from that place—from Grace rather than guilt, from sufficiency rather than scarcity—everything changes. Not overnight. Not magically. But gradually, steadily, powerfully.

Faith, hope, and love aren't just nice spiritual concepts. They're practical tools for building a financial life that actually works—one that supports who you are and who you're called to be.

Key Takeaways

Grace: Remember that you don't have to earn your worth. You already have it.

Faith: Trust your journey and the beliefs and values that guide you, even when progress feels slow.

Hope: Keep looking forward and setting goals that excite you, to balance the ones you think you "should" have.

Love: Center your financial decisions around what truly matters—including your own spiritual and emotional well-being so you can serve others in God's agape love.

In the end, I saw the equation clearly: 100 = 10 + 10 + 80. But more than that, I saw Grace = Faith + Hope + Love. This wasn't just a principle. It was a path—and it's one you can walk with accompaniment.

In the next chapter, we'll explore heritage—how to leave a lasting impact through your financial choices, ensuring that your values continue long after you're gone.

Questions to Consider

Where in your financial life are you operating from fear instead of faith?

What would change if you truly believed you were given life to deploy what you're building to share the love of Grace with others?

How can faith, hope, and love reflect the Grace you've been given and how does this guide your next financial decision?

Chapter 22

Honor the Heritage of Grace

My wife is no longer physically by my side, but Melede's heart and heritage is vibrant. The way we lived, returned, saved, and loved continue in my life as sacrifices that I hope are fragrant to the Lord as my prayers and worship ascend to the Father of Lights. I share this opportunity with you, so you are encouraged to consider if Heritage Habits of Grace are for your benefit and for the benefit of many.

Melede's dedication to me and mine to her was a hallmark of our relationship. We recognized that our love was a gift of divine Grace, since we'd both been praying for a lifetime companion that would be suitable for us.

Melede had saved some money which helped us purchase our first washer and dryer. She worked hard to help us earn money until our first child was born. After that, we were able to curtail our spending on things that were not conducive to family life.

We were able to purchase our first home which gave us the equity or sale value over cost so that we were able then to purchase our homes to come. By now, we kept a strict spending pattern, but made it through these days with joy in our hearts and a closeness that would grow each year.

As time rolled by, the children grew up, had their own families and Melede was called home to be with God. When she left, The Spirit of Grace comforted me as I continued our normal pattern seeking and relying on the Hands of eternal Grace as I worship.

Our decisions for giving, saving, and loving didn't just shape our now—it shaped what she left behind-Grace-always and forever!

What Will You Leave Behind?

You may have spent years navigating the ups and downs of life. You may have worked hard, made tough decisions, built savings, and figured out how to make ends meet. But have you ever stopped to think about the heritage you've received and the one you're creating? What will people remember about you when you're gone? Whatever you do with the material things of life, please make sure that you give them Grace!

How will your life's choices reflect the values you hold dear?

Here's what matters most: Heritage isn't just about the wealth you leave behind. It's about the impact that divine Grace has made on you, and as a reflection of that image, bear the flow and glow of Grace to others. Grace expressed through faith, hope and love will matter in the lives of others through the values you pass down through generations.

Understanding Heritage

Heritage is bigger than your bank account. It's the entirety of your existence—the dreams you chased, the relationships you built, the wisdom you shared, and the generosity given to you from above as well as the values you lived by. It's the story you leave behind, written not in dollars and cents but in love, kindness, mercy, justice, and faith, equivalent to the Grace given to us by God.

Think about the heritage you received from your parents or grandparents. Maybe they taught you the value of hard work, the importance of honoring God, or the significance of living within your means. Their choices shaped how you understand money and life. Those are Heritage Habits!

Now it's your turn to create a heritage—one that reflects your faith, values, and hopes for those who come after you.

Your Financial Choices Create Ripples

Every financial decision you make sends ripples into the world around you. Whether it's how you give, spend, save, or invest, these choices profoundly influence not just your life but the lives of those you care about.

1. Spending with Purpose

Consider how you spend your money. Does it align with your values? When you spend with intention, you communicate what matters to you.

If you care about sustainability, supporting eco-friendly businesses and efforts to steward creation sends a message about your priorities. If you value education, investing in books and learning for your family shows what you believe in. If faithfulness to God is central to your life, your spending hopefully reflects that commitment.

Purposeful spending sets an example for those around you, showing them that financial choices can reflect personal beliefs.

2. Saving for Future Generations

Saving isn't just about accumulating wealth—it's about preparing opportunities for those who come after you. Whether you're setting up a college fund for your grandkids, investing in a family business, or simply ensuring your loved ones have financial security, your savings can become a springboard for their success.

Imagine your children or grandchildren being able to pursue their dreams without the crushing burden of debt. When you prioritize giving and saving, you give them a head start and show them the value of planning ahead.

3. Giving Back

One of the most powerful ways to create a lasting heritage is through returning that reflects the generosity of Grace. How you choose to give—whether through time, talent, or money—all contribute to the significant impact that Grace has on your community and beyond.

Think about the initiatives and organizations that align with your beliefs. Whether it's your church, education, healthcare, mercy ministries, stewardship of creation, or justice work, your offerings help make the world a better place where light shines. By instilling a sense of returning in your family, you set the stage for a heritage of compassion and a reflection of God's generosity.

Planning Your Heritage: Practical Steps

Building and transferring the heritage you want requires intentional planning. It is more than simply what you leave behind—it's about what light you want to illuminate and for what do you want to be remembered. Here are some practical steps:

1. Define Your Priorities and Values

Before you can plan to transfer your heritage, reflect on your core beliefs and values. What truths do you want to guide your decisions? This might include faithfulness, integrity, kindness, generosity, reconciliation, or education. Once you've identified your values and goals, let these beliefs inform your financial choices moving forward.

2. Establish a Will and Estate Gift Plan

Having a will and estate gift plan ensures your wishes are honored after you're gone. This legal documentation lets you specify who you want to have represent you and how you want your assets distributed, making sure they align with your values. Consider working with a charitable planner, a financial advisor and estate planning attorney to navigate this process. Find out what the full scope of planning entails and identify the most effective way to transfer the assets and values you manage.

3. Communicate with Your Loved Ones

Your heritage doesn't rely solely on your financial choices—it's also about the conversations you have. Engage your family in discussions about your values and plans. Help them understand the intentions behind your choices. Encourage open dialogue about money and teach them to make informed financial decisions.

4. Give While You Live

One powerful way to leave a heritage is through giving while you're still alive. Consider setting up a charitable or family gift fund, sponsoring scholarships, or donating to organizations you care about. By giving now, you can see the positive impact of your contributions and inspire others to get involved.

Crafting Your Heritage Story

Your heritage is essentially a story—one that reflects who you are, whose you are and what you stand for. Here's how to shape that story:

1. Ground Yourself in Faith

Your beliefs about God, life, and eternity will shape everything else. Whatever your faith tradition, these beliefs will trigger how you act and what values you prioritize. The God of the Bible has revealed His Name, His nature, and His promises consistently throughout history. Let your faith be the foundation of the heritage you have received, held and will one-day transfer.

2. Document Your Journey

Take time to write down or record your thoughts, experiences, and the lessons you've learned throughout your life. This could be a journal, blog, video, or even letters to your loved ones. By documenting your journey, you create a tangible representation of your struggles, beliefs, and values, allowing future generations to learn from your experiences. This could be as simple as writing a family letter to honor your heritage.

3. Share Your Wisdom

Pass down your knowledge to younger generations. This might involve mentoring someone, teaching financial literacy, or simply having honest conversations about faith, values, and money with your family. Sharing your wisdom creates a bridge between generations if you can share the way of Grace.

4. Create a Family Mission Statement

Gather your family to create a mission statement that captures your shared values and aspirations. This collaborative effort can be a powerful bonding experience and a guide for future decisions. A clear mission statement serves as a reminder of the Grace heritage you're building together, according to God's good and perfect will.

The Heart of Heritage: Faith, Relationships, and Values

Leaving a heritage is intimate, spiritual, and emotional. It's about the connections forged by faith and hope, the love you've received and then shared, and the impact you've had on others. The Holy Spirit of Grace is the giver of our eternal heritage. May our Heritage Habits of Grace be as we have received with increase.

The Faith that Nurtures

Faith is a top priority for countless people worldwide. Whatever you learn about God and His nature as a child will likely stay with you. Hopefully, the tenets of your belief system encourage rather than defeat you. Your faith shapes your decisions in life and how you approach the end of life. As we draw closer to God, let us remember that His nature as revealed in Jesus is Grace; sufficient for the day and sufficient for eternity.

The Relationships that Build

Your relationships begin with the Grace of God. That Grace is shared with others as a vital part of your heritage. How you treat others, the time you spend with loved ones, and the support you provide all contribute to the memories you leave behind and the flow of Grace to others. Prioritize meaningful connections and make sure those you love to know how much they matter.

The Beliefs and Values Instilled

The beliefs and values you embody and pass down create a heritage that extends beyond financial wealth. Whether it's forgiveness and reconciliation, honesty, kindness, or perseverance, instilling these values in your family and community shapes their lives for years to come.

The Stories You Share

Your life is filled with stories—moments of triumph, hardship, joy, and love. Share these stories with your family, encouraging them to carry the narrative forward. By sharing your experiences, you give them a deeper understanding of who you are and what you represent.

"Heritage is Grace transferred to and shared with our children's, children's, children."

Teaching Financial Wisdom

One of the most useful heritages you can leave is financial education. Equip your loved ones with the knowledge and skills they need to navigate their own financial journeys confidently. Teach them the Economies of Grace which are contained in the Holy Bible.

1. Open Discussions About Money

Create an environment where talking about money is normal. Discuss budgeting, giving, saving, investing, and making informed decisions. This openness helps demystify finances and encourages healthy conversations about resources. It helps to model discipline and diligence, to strengthen ties.

2. Teach Practical Skills

Teach those under your care practical financial skills—budgeting techniques, how to read a credit report, savings, and investment strategies. By providing them with these resources, you equip them to manage their financial futures in a way that is equivalent and faithful to Grace.

3. Lead by Example

Your actions speak louder than words. Demonstrate good financial patterns in your own life—give to honor Grace, save regularly, avoid debt if possible and invest wisely. When your loved ones see you practicing what you preach, they're more likely to adopt similar behaviors.

Creating Impact Through Love that Flows from Grace

Charitable giving is a powerful way to create lasting impact. It has always been a practice to honor the object of our obedience and worship.

Here's how to incorporate giving into your heritage plan:

1. Identify Causes You Care About

Reflect on the causes that resonate with you—faith, education, healthcare, mercy and benevolent work, social justice, the environment. Identifying these causes helps you direct your resources toward making a difference in areas you're passionate about.

2. Research Charitable Organizations

Once you've identified your causes, search like-minded communities and see those out that align with your beliefs and spiritual values. Look for those with a proven track record of making the world a better place. This alignment with faith ensures your contributions have aligned and meaningful impact.

3. Consider a Charitable Gift Fund

If you're passionate about giving, consider establishing a charitable gift fund or donor-advised fund. This allows you to support causes systematically and provides a platform for future generations to continue your charitable vision.

Heritage Habits Beyond Money

Remember, your heritage is about more than just money. It's about the love you've received and share, the kindness you've received and show, and the values you live by and instill.

Emotional Wealth

Your emotional wealth—how you connect with others and the relationships you nurture—will be remembered long after your possessions are gone. Prioritize emotional connections and invest yourself in the people you care about.

Time and Presence

Time is one of the most valuable gifts you can offer. Be present for your loved ones, share experiences, forgive, and absolve, create memories. Your presence will be felt even when you're no longer there.

Inspire Future Generations

Your heritage in Grace can inspire others to make helpful changes in their lives and communities. Whether through acts of kindness, community service, or living by Grace values, your influence extends beyond your lifetime.

What beliefs and values do you want to give to the lives of others?

Building a Grace Heritage Now

As you navigate your financial journey, remember that every choice you make contributes to the way in which the Grace Heritage you've received flows to others. From how you give, spend, and save to the values you instill and the resulting connections you nurture, your responses to Grace shape the story you leave behind. If Grace warms your life, let it glow so others flourish under her warmth.

Consider the impact you want to make and take intentional steps to build a heritage that reflects the eternal light of divine Grace. Whether through purposeful spending, thoughtful giving, or nurturing relationships, your heritage is a testament to the life you've lived, and the difference Grace makes in the world as you continue to live in Grace and reflect it.

Now, ask yourself:

- How do you want to be remembered?
- What steps can you take today to ensure your heritage resonates long after you're gone?
- What heritage do you hope reflects your vision of the full life for you and your loved ones, for generations to come?

Your financial decisions can leave behind a lasting benefit, ensuring that your ardent values continue to equip, inspire, and uplift future generations.

The time to start building that heritage is now.

Chapter 23

Your 100% Life Starts Now

This journey changed me. The 100% Life isn't defined by numbers, yet the God of Order has given His Word as a light to our paths, which helps us live in Grace. In faith. In hope. In love.

When I started as a kid, I had big dreams but no roadmap. I couldn't have told you where my life would go—only that I wanted it to matter.

What I learned early was discipline. My family taught me that staying in God's Word was like building a house on solid rock instead of sand. Those foundation stones—worship, prayer, study, reading, listening, thinking—would help me weather any storm. But back then, my ambition was focused: be everything I was created to be.

Looking back, I held my first part-time job in the 5th grade. Yes, fifth grade. Child labor laws were apparently more flexible back then. I worked partly to help my dad with expenses and partly to buy the things kids want—probably ice cream treats, baseball cards, or sports equipment, if I'm honest. The pattern stuck: work hard, be diligent, take responsibility seriously. But here's the truth—my heart was still hard. I was focused on *my* wants, *my* needs, *my* stuff.

Then marriage and kids arrived, and that ushered in a new era. Suddenly, responsibility wasn't just about me anymore. Grace helped me to want to use my abilities to reflect the Grace that I'd been given—not in tiny drops, but in sufficient, flowing quantities.

I owe everything to the God of Grace, who gave me life, redeemed my flawed person to be acceptable before a perfect God, and daily provides all good things. My God sent His Spirit of Grace to create and strengthen my faith. This blessed gift of faith allows me to trust the One who Created and Redeemed me. Grace is the lamb of God who takes away the sins of the world (John 1:29 ESV). And honestly? There's deep comfort in knowing God walks with us through it all to save and not condemn.

Over time, I found real satisfaction in my vocation as a teacher and counselor, even when the paycheck didn't quite stretch to cover a growing family's needs. There were months when our budget was tighter than a new pair of dress shoes).

As I grew older, I learned to understand why returning and saving mattered as much as earning.

When these pieces started aligning with Grace, something unexpected happened for me—spending naturally contracted to fit within our income. Not because we were gritting our teeth and white-knuckling it, but because we were living intentionally.

We pressed forward even when storm clouds gathered. We realized that God's Grace isn't just sufficient for today—wonder of wonders, it's made perfect in our weakness until the end of time. That part of my journey changed me.

The 100% Life isn't just about numbers. It's about hearing the calling to live each day so the gifts of your faith, hope, and love shine and glow. It's about God's eternal and daily Grace in us.

And God's Grace is more than enough.

Bringing it All Together

We're approaching the end of our journey through *The Grace Formula.* You've taken a deep dive into managing life and all its resources as a steward. You've discovered how Grace can be both anchor and compass—guiding your decisions to reflect faith, hope, and love.

Whether you're giving to meet others' needs or honor the God of all Grace, taking on debt for a home or car, saving for the future, investing in your community, or thinking about your heritage, each choice is an opportunity. You get to live a life that's full, grounded, caring, intentional, and aligned with your deepest beliefs and values. If your life flows through Grace, then let it shine, let it flow, let it glow!

Maybe you're 25-30 right now, navigating family or career, trying to pay off student loans, or just figuring out how to build the life you want. Perhaps money feels like a constant stress point or an elusive goal, always a few steps ahead. Or maybe it feels like a leaking hose with nothing left until next payday (I've been there. We've all been there).

Here's what I want you to remember: It's not about being perfect or having it all figured out right away. It's about taking small steps and making consistent choices rooted in the belief that there is Grace in your journey and Grace *for* your journey. Every dollar you earn and spend reflects something about you—your dreams, your priorities, your hope, love, and faith.

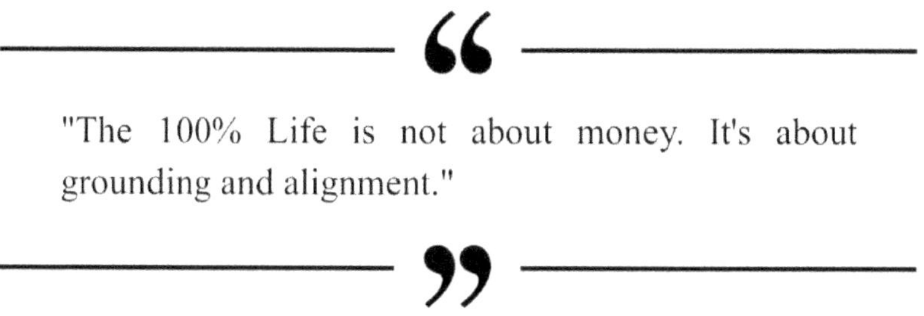

Key Takeaways: Living with Purpose

Faith, Hope, and Love in Financial Stewardship

As you navigate life's changes, remember that financial management is more than spreadsheets and numbers. When you recognize that your resources, though limited, are enough in Grace, you are much more open to learning to live within your means.

It's about having faith in God's provision, being prudent, confident, and bold for the future, and love for others that shines through your stewardship.

Returning/tithing, saving, and living as a "soul of blessing" isn't just about economic virtue or good works. They are identity and purpose granted in Holy Baptism, anchoring or grounding your life to true meaning. These actions balance your decision patterns—with what you understand to be equivalent to Grace.

The Power of Small Choices

Even the smallest financial decisions can have an enduring or abiding impact. Your spending plan or budgeting, establishing and building an emergency savings fund, and living within limits while setting aside money for the future are ways to set yourself up for victory. But more importantly, each decision becomes an act of discipline and faith.

Each choice adds up. Over time, they help you manage life's economic decisions to reflect your values and build a future you're enthusiastic about—one with the stability of divine Grace. If your heart still feels hard, begin asking the God of Grace for softening. Ask to become more pliable, more ready to pivot toward Jubilee.

How Important is a Heritage of Grace?

Heritage. This is a big word, but a simple truth at its core. Heritage is the full life and blessings you've received that you'll one day leave behind. Your economic decisions today create ripple effects for future generations.

Whether it's witnessing that your faith is real, sharing resources with causes that matter, giving with open eyes and a willing heart, or setting up a trust for your family, your choices leave a lasting impact.

Heritage isn't about wealth. It's about how you use resources to bless (not curse) the objects of your love. It's about reflecting values that shine light in darkness, and it's about passing on the heritage of faith, hope, and love, equivalent to Grace.

Recap: The Journey You're On

Let's quickly recap what you've learned:

Understanding Grace: Stewardship begins with recognizing that all resources aren't truly ours—they're all a trust created and funded by God's action in creation and in offering His Son as the unblemished lamb, the perfect sacrifice for a disharmonious world. You've been entrusted with life and resources not just for yourself, but to bear and reflect God's image and thus make the world better. This is the light of the Lord's Jubilee.

Faith in Action: You've explored how faith informs financial decisions—from tithing as an act of trust to embracing hope as motivation for saving and planning. The future in such Grace is bathed in selfless agape love.

Love in Living: Living your 100% life means making choices that reflect lasting love for others. That's supporting family and others to flourish, contributing to charitable organizations that overlap with our mission, and/or building economic stability so you can give with generous eyes.

Honorable Stewardship: We've talked about making financial and economic decisions with integrity, honesty, justice, and mercy—but also with transparency for accountability. How you use time, talent, and money says volumes about who you are, what you stand for, and your stability and consistency.

Heritage Habit Building: Your economic life isn't just about the present—it's about honoring a heritage held together through the ages, by the Grace of God. Heritage Habits that you deploy will bear the image of God's Grace. Whether it is in returning generously, saving and investing with diligence and ensuring your family is cared for in ways that honor them as treasures, today's decisions echo into tomorrow.

Final Words: Stepping Into the Future

As you close this book, I want you to remember something crucial: You are intended to live a life of sufficient Grace—not just in economic or financial terms, but in faith, hope, and love. This journey is ongoing. The lessons here are tools to carry through every stage of life.

Challenges will come. Count on it. Unexpected expenses, tough decisions, moments when you feel alone or like giving up. (Welcome to being human.) But I encourage you to pause, reflect, and remember: stewardship of life and its resources reflects God's heart in yours.

You have Grace within you—the power to shape your story and build something lasting that impacts the world with Light.

If you're ever unsure, remember you don't have to go it alone. We all need help along the way. Maybe you're thinking about how to stabilize income, build that emergency savings fund, invest wisely, or leave a meaningful heritage of Grace.

The 100% Life book series launched with The Grace Formula, and the community @Jubilee Junction LLC offers the power of Grace for you. Discover our curated journey and strategic Grace-grounded teaching and guidance to walk alongside you as you uncover what living at Grace 100% = Faith 10% + Hope 10% + Love 80% truly means.

The journey doesn't end here. It's just beginning.

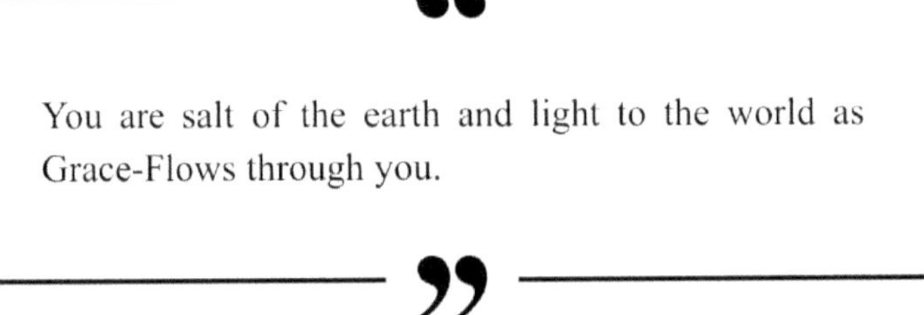

About Philip Meinzen

Philip Meinzen is a third-generation missionary, shaped by a lifetime of faithfully lived roles — son, brother, husband, father, grandfather, teacher, and charitable planning counselor. Raised in India, he carries that heritage into every page of this book.

Grace sustained his wife Melede through ALS and brought her to eternal healing in 2023. Their four children have each flourished in beautifully different ways, and Philip's heritage now extends to eleven grandchildren.

Philip exalts the Lord for Grace in every step of the Journey to Jubilee.

Discover more at www.GraceFlows.org.

About Kim Groshek

Kim Groshek is an executive decision strategist, author, and founder of Human OS™. She helps 7-figure CEOs, founders, and thought leaders turn complex decisions into clear direction—so their businesses can scale without them having to carry everything.

With more than 35 years as a business owner and over 55 published books, Kim's work sits at the intersection of leadership, story, and execution. She is best known for her frameworks on decision integrity and "UN-DECISION"—the hidden cost of decisions that never fully end—and for helping leaders build systems where clarity turns into momentum.

Through her advisory work, interviews with CEOs, and the Thread Media community, Kim guides high-level leaders to translate insight into structure and structure into sustainable results. Her approach blends strategic precision with grounded presence—helping leaders move forward with confidence, authority, and calm.

In *The Grace Formula*, Kim brings a deeper dimension to her work—exploring how Grace, clarity, and decision-making integrity intersect to shape not just outcomes, but the way we live, lead, and relate.

Learn more at KimGroshek.com.

More Encouragement

Grace-Flows[SM] Ecosystem

Every steward of the mysteries of God's Grace needs more than a formula—they need a living, breathing community of resources in a movement that meets them where they are and equips them for where God is calling them. The Grace-Flows[SM] movement at @Jubilee Junction™ LLC is that: a growing collection of assessments, design toolkits, curriculum tracks, dialogue and encouragement resources built around the Grace Formula[SM] —Grace (100%) = Faith + Hope + Love[SM] —rooted in the timeless truth of 1 Corinthians 13:13 and Galatians 2:20. Whether you are just beginning to explore what it means to live as a Grace steward or you are ready to go deeper, there is a next step waiting for you.

Scan the QR Code and step into resources designed not to overwhelm, but to orient—helping you discover your placement across the five dimensions of Spirit, Wealth-Vocation, Health, Relationships, and Time. You are not a giver. You are a steward, returning what has already been entrusted to you by a Grace-filled God who loved you first. *"I have been crucified with Christ. It is no longer I who live, but Christ who lives in me. And the life I now live in the flesh I live by faith in the Son of God, who loved me and gave himself for me."* (Galatians 2:20, ESV)

We have included the 15 Biblical Truths for Individual Grace Stewards and the 21 Biblical Truths for Corporate Stewards here. You can find additional resources and enrichment at www.GraceFlows.org.

15 Biblical Truths about Money, Resources, and Grace

The Apostle John describes Jesus as "full of Grace and Truth" (John 1:14 ESV). *"And the Word became flesh and dwelt among us, and we have seen his glory, glory as of the only Son from the Father, full of Grace and Truth."*

That combination matters. Grace without truth becomes mushy sentimentality. Truth without Grace becomes crushing legalism. But together? They form the GPS for your financial journey.

Here's the question that started it all, straight from the Apostle Paul: ***"What do you have that you did not receive? If then you received it, why do you boast as if you did not receive it?"*** (1 Corinthians 4:7 ESV)

That question changes everything. Your brain? Gift. Your talents? Gift. Your opportunities? Gift. Even the next breath you take. Gift. All Grace.

Let's explore 15 foundational truths from God's Word about how eternal Grace shapes the way we think about and decide what to do with money and resources.

1. Everything Belongs to God

Grace is the assurance that everything belongs to God

(Psalm 24:1 ESV) *"The earth is the Lord's and the fullness thereof, the world and those who dwell therein."*

Every breath. Every dollar. Every minute. Every skill you have—all gifts of Grace. You're not the owner. You're the caretaker.

I used to think the money I earned from my jobs was all mine. I worked for it, right? Then God opened my eyes to see that Grace gave me the ability, strength, and opportunity to do the work in the first place.

That perspective shift changed our decision-making. When you realize everything is a gift, you stop white-knuckling your resources and start stewarding them with open hands.

2. You Are a Steward—A Caretaker

Grace encourages you to take up your role as a steward

(1 Corinthians 4:2, Genesis 2:15 ESV 2 Corinthians 6:1) "*Moreover, it is required of stewards that they be found faithful.*" *"The Lord God took the man and put him in the garden of Eden to work it and keep it."*

The very first job description in the Bible? Caretaker. God placed Adam in the Garden of Eden "to work it and keep it." Translation: take care of this beautiful life I'm entrusting to you. Protect it. Help it flourish.

When I cared for my neighbor's garden and fish tanks while she was away, I treated them exactly as she requested—not how I would have done it. That's how Grace wants us to handle what we've been given. Use it wisely. Care for it well. Help everything and everyone under your care become all that Grace intended.

3. Grace Provides What You Need

Grace promises to give us our 'Daily Bread' or everything we need for this body and life.
(Philippians 4:19 ESV) "*And my God will supply every need of yours according to his riches in glory in Christ Jesus.*"

Notice it says *need*, not necessarily *want*. There's a difference between needing transportation and wanting a luxury sports car. (One gets you to work. The other gets you noticed at stoplights.)

When I was in college—broke and scrambling—I prayed for a way to make money. The next day, a friend told me about a job opening. That was Grace's provision. Not a lottery win. Not a miracle inheritance. Just the right opportunity at the right time.

4. Be Content with What You Have

Grace encourages and equips you to be content

(Hebrews 13:5 ESV) *"Keep your life free from love of money, and be content with what you have, for he has said, 'I will never leave you nor forsake you.'"*

Contentment means feeling grateful for what you have rather than anxious about what you don't. It's finding peace in enough.

I once desperately wanted a fancy Swiss watch. Convinced myself I *needed* it. Then I realized my old watch worked perfectly fine. Some years later, with the advent of smartphones, I stopped wearing watches altogether.

Turns out I didn't need it at all. Less stuff, more peace.

5. Money Can Trick You

Riches can be deceptive

(1 Timothy 6:10 ESV) *"For the love of money is a root of all kinds of evils. It's through this craving that some have wandered away from the faith and pierced themselves with many pangs.'*

Money itself isn't evil—it's the *love* of money that causes problems. Money can bless or curse you, depending on your relationship with it.

I've known people who were wealthy but miserable because they chased riches over relationships, valued control over service, failed to pass on their values, and carry a sense of guilt. What you chase shapes who you become. Chase the wind, reap the whirlwind. Worship created things as a deity irrupts a spiritual storm that pushes your drift from your Creator. But if your heart is anchored in Grace, your decisions lead to a contrite recognition of being disconnected from your Source of Grace. The Holy Spirit helps you find your true identity and meaning in Divine Grace.

6. Take Care of What You've Been Given

Exercise faithful stewardship or management

(Luke 16:10 ESV) *"One who is faithful in a very little is also faithful in much."*

Don't waste the money, time, or skills you've been given. I blew far too many paychecks on frivolous stuff in my younger years and regret it. Those things left me feeling empty.

Start by valuing every resource—even the small ones—as opportunities to be faithful. How you handle five dollars reveals how you'll handle five thousand.

7. Increase What You Have

Increase what's entrusted to you

(Matthew 25:14-30 ESV) *Parable of the Talents vs. 29- "For to everyone who has will more be given, and he will have an abundance. Burt from the one who has not, even what he has will be taken away."*

In Jesus' parable of the talents, the servants who increased what they were given got rewarded. The one who buried his talent in the backyard? Not so much. Gracc, as thc Mastcr, cxpccts confidcnt initiative, not fearful defensiveness.

Grace expects us to grow resources boldly and wisely to reflect

Grace given to me. When I started teaching, money was tight. I wasn't saving adequately. Then I helped a friend with his landscaping business one summer.

Turns out I had a knack for it—maybe inherited from my grandfather, who painted landscapes, or my mother, who had an artist's eye. Either way, I started a small landscaping business, enjoying using a shovel as my paintbrush. It grew to three crews.

The extra income helped with a new wife and kids, but it also taught me the joy of purposeful work. There's something deeply satisfying about seeing people value things that beautify their lives. When I noticed this, I also noticed that people didn't show the same appreciation for the beauty of the Word of God in our midst. But I digress.

8. Sufficiency Is Meant for Sharing

Share in the Flow of Grace

(2 Corinthians 9:8 ESV) *"And God is able to make all Grace abound to you, so that having all sufficiency in all things, at all times, you may abound in every good work."*

When you have more than you need, you have an opportunity to bless others.

During my youth in rural South India, I helped my family feed hundreds of hungry, malnourished people with simple rice and powdered milk. Their gratitude filled me more than anything I could have returned to them.

Sharing what you have and returning what you've been given multiplies its meaning.

9. Give God Your Best First

Return the God of Grace, your first fruits

(Proverbs 3:9-10 ESV) *"Honor the Lord with your wealth and with the first fruits of all your produce."*

Honor Grace with the first and best of what you have—your time, money, and energy. Even when money was tight for me, giving first taught me to trust Grace for the rest.

This release transforms giving from an obligation into an act of worship that brought me fullness, peace, and joy.

10. Return Because You Want To

Return from the heart, willingly

(2 Corinthians 9:7 ESV) *"God loves a cheerful giver."*

Return with a happy heart, not just because you feel you should. There were times when I returned out of obligation, and it left me feeling empty. But when I learned to return with childlike faith in the generosity first given to me through Grace, I felt liberated.

Here's the paradox: returning often benefits the returner more than the receiver. After 30 years of helping people with charitable returns planning, I've witnessed the obvious joy in their lives. As you reflect glowing flows of Grace's generosity, it does something transformative for your soul.

11. Show Kindness to Those in Need

Grace requires kindness to the poor

(Proverbs 19:17 ESV) *"Whoever is generous to the poor lends to the Lord, and he will repay him for his deed."*

I once met a man, a little older than me, who hadn't eaten all day. His life was completely broken, and he wasn't able to provide for himself. My heart had compassion on him. I realized that, except for different circumstances, this could be me.

I shared a meal with him and gave him some money for his journey. Grace reminds us to walk humbly—we might be entertaining angels without knowing it. (See Hebrews 13:2 if you think I'm making that up.)

12. Practice God's Generosity with Gratitude

Rejoice in and exult the God of all Grace

(Philippians 4:4-7 ESV) *"Rejoice in the Lord always... Do not be anxious about anything, but in everything by prayer and supplication with thanksgiving let your requests be made known to God."*

Gratitude transforms your perspective. Each night, I express thanks for the day's blessings. Even on tough days, I ask for mercy. This practice keeps my heart anchored in reconciled, liberating Grace.

There's no better way to recognize your dependence on Grace than with a humble, contrite, grateful spirit.

13. Don't Let Debt Enslave You

Borrowing obligates your future

(Romans 13:8, Proverbs 22:7 ESV) *"Owe no one anything, except to love each other." "The borrower is servant to the lender."*

Debt feels like carrying a heavy backpack everywhere you go. It weighs you down, slows you down, and reminds you it's there with every step.

When you borrow money, you're also borrowing against your future freedom. I've used credit cards for things I could have saved for, then spent years paying them off—with interest. (Turns out, credit card companies are very good at math. Very, very good.)

Living within your means brings financial stability and freedom. Grace warns us not to be enslaved by debt that steals tomorrow's peace.

14. Save Some of What You Earn

Save wisely with Hope.

(Proverbs 21:20 ESV) *"Precious treasure and oil are in a wise man's dwelling, but a foolish man devours it."*

Saving isn't about fearing the future—it's about being wisely prepared for it. Living on less than you earn is a discipline that builds financial integrity.

My emergency savings fund let me buy reliable transportation so my friends and I could get to work across town. Plus, we enjoyed the rides together—singing off-key to the radio and solving the world's problems during the commute.

Preparation brings peace.

15. Be Trustworthy with What You're Given

Practice stewardship or management faithful to the Grace that Gives

(1 Corinthians 4:2 ESV) *"Moreover, it is required of stewards that they be found faithful or trustworthy."*

Grace requires integrity—managing decisions in alignment with God's promises.

Here's the beautiful paradox: Grace's perfect nature calls for our best effort in all we do, yet loves us completely in our imperfect, earthly humanity. To those who prove trustworthy with a little, more is entrusted.

The Bottom Line

These 15 truths form the anchor of a Grace-grounded approach to money and

resources. They're not rules to burden you—they're wisdom to free you.

When you embrace these principles, something shifts inside. You move from anxiety to

Contentment. From scarcity to gratitude for sufficiency. From ownership to stewardship.

You discover what it means to live your 100% life—where **Grace = Faith + Hope + Love**SM also expressed as **Grace (100%) = Faith (10%) + Hope (10%) + Love (80%)**SM

Here is your invitation: join the journey of understanding that Grace is sufficient. When you recognize and accept in humility that everything you have is a gift, everything changes.

Not just your bank account. Not just your budget. *Everything.*

21 Biblical Truths for Corporate Fiscal Stewardship

Core Biblical Truths with Descriptions

1. Grace Wants Your Ministry Free from the Bondage of Debt (Truth 1) *"Let no debt remain outstanding, except the continuing debt to love one another." —Romans 13:8*

Scripture consistently equates debt with slavery and positions it as a curse for disobedience. Freedom from debt is presented as a blessing promised to those who obey the Lord, enabling ministries to be lenders rather than borrowers, the head rather than the tail. Biblical teaching advocates rejecting debt entirely, not as lack of faith, but as alignment with God's design for financial freedom.

2. Grace Encourages You to Save for the Future (Truth 2) *"Go to the ant, you sluggard, consider its way and be wise! It has no commander, no overseer or ruler, yet it stores its provisions in summer and gathers its food at harvest." —Proverbs 6:6–8*

Following the example of the wise ant in Proverbs, ministries should store provisions during times of plenty to survive times of scarcity. Being the "lender to nations" requires first having something to lend, which necessitates systematic saving rather than plate-to-plate existence.

3. Grace Calls Us to Provide for God's Servants and the Poor (Truth 3) *"At the end of every three years, bring all the tithes of that year's produce and store it in your towns, so that the Levites (who have no allotment or inheritance of their own) and the aliens, the fatherless and the widows who live in your towns may come and eat and be satisfied." —Deuteronomy 14:28-29*

One-third of Israel's tithes were stored locally in food banks to feed Levitical priests serving outside Jerusalem and to provide for foreigners, orphans, and widows. This sacred portion represented the first-fruits—the very best the land produced—reserved specifically for missionaries and the vulnerable.

4. Grace Calls Us to Build Ministry Treasuries (Truths 4-5) *"He gave him the plans of all that the Spirit had put in his mind for the courts of the temple of the LORD and all the surrounding rooms, for the treasuries of the temple of God and for the treasuries for the dedicated things." —1 Chronicles 28:12*

God's inspired design for the temple included multiple separate treasuries: storerooms, treasuries of the temple of God, and treasuries for dedicated things. Separate treasuries prevented commingling of funds and ensured offerings given for different purposes remained segregated and were used exclusively as designated.

5. Grace Teaches Us to Save Before Building (Truth 6) *"They received from Moses all the offerings the Israelites had brought to carry out the work of constructing the sanctuary." —Exodus 36:3*

From the tabernacle in the wilderness to Solomon's temple to Nehemiah's walls, biblical building projects began only after fundraising was complete. Jesus himself taught the wisdom of counting the cost and having funds on hand before starting construction to avoid the ridicule of unfinished projects.

6. Grace Leads Us to Establish Facility Operations and Repair Funds (Truth 7) *"Some of the plunder taken in battle they dedicated for the repair of the temple of the LORD." —1 Chronicles 26:27*

King David set aside dedicated funds for temple repair before the temple was even built, demonstrating proactive planning to prevent deferred maintenance. This endowed treasury ensured perpetual resources for ongoing facility operations and capital repairs.

7. Grace Invites Us to Fund Treasuries Through Dedicated Gifts (Truth 8) *"A priest descended from Aaron is to accompany the Levites when they receive the tithes, and the Levites are to bring a tenth of the tithes up to the house of our God, to the storerooms of the treasury." —Nehemiah 10:38*

Treasuries of dedicated items were funded by freewill offerings specifically dedicated to God for particular purposes (restricted gifts) and by the "tithe of the tithe"—the Levites' offering of one-tenth of the tithes they received, representing the best and holiest portion reserved exclusively for the Lord.

8. Grace Empowers Us to Endow Dedicated Funds (Truth 9) *"I walk in the way of righteousness, along the paths of justice, bestowing wealth on those who love me and making their treasuries full." —Proverbs 8:20–21*

The Lord's portion (tithe of the tithe) could not be distributed or spent but was invested to generate perpetual income. These funds were lent only to foreigners (not fellow Israelites), positioning Israel as lender to nations and creating an ever-growing stream of investment income.

9. Grace Guides Us to Preserve Principal (Truth 10) *"If you do whatever I command you and walk in my ways and do what is right in my eyes by keeping my statutes and commands, as David my servant did, I will be with you. I will build you a dynasty as enduring as the one I built for David." —1 Kings 11:38*

"The principled preserve principal"—only investment income from endowed funds should be spent, never the principal itself. Consuming principal is like killing the goose that lays golden eggs or burning the branches of a fruit-bearing tree; both stop producing.

10. Grace Prepares Us to Build Great Endowments for Great Crises (Truth 11) *"Thus Joseph stored up grain in great abundance like the sand of the sea, until he stopped measuring it, for it was beyond measure." —Genesis 41:49*

Noah's ark and Joseph's grain warehouses demonstrate that emergency times call for emergency measures. When crisis looms, God's people should build endowments "beyond measure"—Noah saved over 100 years; Joseph warehoused 20% of seven years' harvest.

11. Grace Enables Us to Receive Testamentary Bequests (Truth 12) *"Over and above everything I have provided for this holy temple, I now give my personal treasures of gold and silver for the temple of my God." —1 Chronicles 29:3*

King David's estate plan demonstrates the power of planned giving. He created a charitable trust with restricted gifts for temple construction and endowment, then used his lead pledge as a challenge gift that leveraged matching donations from Israel's leaders, multiplying the impact exponentially.

12. Grace Opens the Estate Return Planning Opportunity (Truth 13) *"This is what the LORD says: Put your house in order, because you are going to die." —2 Kings 20:1*

Current demographic and wealth transfer trends present unprecedented opportunities for ministries to receive testamentary gifts from aging supporters if return mindset planning structures and encouragement are in place. This calls for charitable planners representing the ministry to be involved in the planning process for stewards.

13. Grace Challenges Us to Build Generational Treasuries (Truth 14) *"The city and all that is in it are to be devoted to the LORD ... All the silver and gold and the articles of bronze and iron are sacred to the LORD and must go into his treasury." —Joshua 6:19*

Ministry treasuries were designed to last for generations, from Joshua through Christ's time. They provided continuity through conquest, exile, restoration, and beyond—demonstrating the importance of building financial structures that transcend individual lifetimes.

14. Grace Directs Us to Diversify Investments (Truth 15) *"Hezekiah had very great riches and honor, and he made treasuries for his silver and gold and for his precious stones, spices, shields and all kinds of valuables." —2 Chronicles 32:27*

Scripture shows ministry treasuries holding diverse assets: precious metals, livestock, grain, wine, oil, and other valuables—each requiring separate storage. This diversification protected against single-point failures and matched different assets to appropriate uses.

15. Grace Shows Us the Value of Supporting Organizations (Truth 16) *"Their fellow Levites were in charge of the treasuries of the house of God and the treasuries for the dedicated things. Jehieli and his sons were in charge of the treasuries of the temple of the LORD. Shelomoth and his relatives were in charge of all the treasuries of the things dedicated." —1 Chronicles 26:20, 22, 26*

Separating endowed funds into dedicated treasuries managed by separate teams of treasurers (not single individuals) prevented misappropriation, misfeasance, and theft while improving accountability and removing temptation through distributed oversight.

16. Grace Points Us to Professional Management (Truth 17) *"Hezekiah gave orders to prepare storerooms in the temple of the LORD, and this was done. Then they faithfully brought in the contributions, tithes and dedicated gifts." —2 Chronicles 31:11-12*

Named treasurers with specific responsibilities managed Israel's complex treasury system. Professional expertise was essential for collecting, counting, storing, protecting, investing, and properly distributing the various offerings according to their designated purposes.

17. Grace Justifies Paying for Professional Help (Truth 18) *"You may use the silver for whatever you wish—cattle, sheep, wine or other fermented drink, or anything else you desire. There you shall eat in the presence of the LORD your God and rejoice." —Deuteronomy 14:26*

Quality stewardship of significant resources justifies compensating qualified professionals to build and manage endowments properly, ensuring faithful administration of sacred trusts.

18. Grace Counsels Us to Retain Multiple Advisers (Truth 19) *"Plans fail for lack of counsel, but with many advisers they succeed." —Proverbs 15:22*

Proverbs teaches the wisdom of seeking counsel from many advisers. Complex treasury management, investment decisions, and charitable planning benefit from diverse professional perspectives.

19. Grace Provides Budget-Neutral Funding Methods (Truth 20) *"According to their ability they gave to the treasury for this work." —Ezra 2:69*

Creative and intentional approaches can fund professional help without impacting current operations—such as dedicating portions of bequests specifically to cover endowment management costs or using initial investment income for administrative expenses.

20. Grace Requires Clergy Involvement (Truth 21) *"A priest descended from Aaron is to accompany the Levites when they receive the tithes." —Nehemiah 10:38*

Priests accompanied Levites when receiving tithes and oversaw treasury operations. Pastoral engagement ensures theological alignment, maintains accountability, and keeps ministry focus central to financial decision-making.

Simple Scripture List

Commands and Examples:

- Bring tithes to ministry treasuries (Malachi 3:10; Nehemiah 10:38-39)
- Store one-third of tithes for Levites and the poor (Deuteronomy 14:28-29; 26:12-13)
- Levites offer tithe of the tithe—the Lord's portion (Numbers 18:26-29)
- Separate treasuries for separate purposes (1 Chronicles 26:20-26)
- Separate teams manage separate treasuries (1 Chronicles 26:22-28)
- Save before building (Exodus 36:3-7; 1 Chronicles 29:2-9)
- Dedicate funds for future repairs (1 Chronicles 26:27; 2 Chronicles 31:11-12)
- Let no debt remain outstanding (Romans 13:8)
- Blessing: lend to nations, not borrow (Deuteronomy 15:4-6; 28:12-13)
- Curse: borrower is slave to lender (Proverbs 22:7; Deuteronomy 28:43-45)

Wisdom Teachings:

- Consider the ant—store provisions (Proverbs 6:6-8)
- Count the cost before building (Luke 14:28-30)
- Be prepared likewise virgins (Matthew 25:1-13)
- Faithful stewards increase master's property (Matthew 25:14-30; Luke 19:12-27)
- Charge foreigners' interest, not brothers (Deuteronomy 23:19-20)
- Sacred portions must remain sacred (Deuteronomy 26:13-14)
- Give first-fruits, not leftovers (Deuteronomy 26:2; Nehemiah 10:35-37)

Historical Examples:

- Joshua established first treasury (Joshua 6:19, 24)
- David received inspired plans for treasuries (1 Chronicles 28:11-12)
- Solomon filled ministry treasuries (1 Kings 7:51)
- Hezekiah built storerooms (2 Chronicles 31:11)
- Nehemiah/Ezra rededicated treasuries (Nehemiah 12:44; 13:4-13)
- Widow's offering to ministry treasury (Mark 12.41-44)
- Noah's ark endowment (Genesis 6:21-22)
- Joseph's grain endowment (Genesis 41:33-36, 47-49)
- David's estate plan and challenge pledge (1 Chronicles 29:1-9)

Consequences of Misuse:

- Asa raided treasuries, rebuked for faithlessness (2 Chronicles 16:2-9)
- Joash emptied treasuries, later assassinated (2 Kings 12:18)
- Hezekiah stripped temple, invasion continued (2 Kings 18:14-16)
- Achan stole banned items, brought curse (Joshua 7:1-26)

Principles:

- All Scripture is God-breathed and useful (2 Timothy 3:16-17)
- God's thoughts/ways differ from ours (Isaiah 55:8-9)
- Different members, one body (Romans 12:4-5; 1 Corinthians 12:27)
- Perfect love casts out fear (1 John 4:18)
- In everything give thanks (1 Thessalonians 5:18)

www.ingramcontent.com/pod-product-compliance
Lightning Source LLC
LaVergne TN
LVHW020706110826
845149LV00012B/2132

* 9 7 9 8 9 9 9 8 7 9 6 2 2 *